Most Southerners who fought in the Civil War were native born, white, and Confederate. However, thousands with other ethnic backgrounds also took a stand—and not always for the South. *Invisible Southerners* recounts the wartime experiences of the region's German Americans, Native Americans, and African Americans. As Anne J. Bailey looks at how such outsiders responded to demands on their loyalties, she recaptures the atmosphere of suspicion in which they strove to understand, and be understood by, their proslavery, secessionist neighbors.

Divisions within groups complicated circumstances even after members had cast their lot with the Union or Confederacy. Europe's slavery-free legacy swayed many German Americans against the Confederacy. Even so, a pro-Union German soldier could look askance at another who was from a different province in the Old Country or of a different religious sect. Creeks and Cherokees faced wartime questions made thornier by tribal rifts based on wealth, racial mixture, and bitter memories of their forced transport to the Indian Territory decades earlier. Choosing sides was easiest for former slaves, says Bailey, but the consequences were more dire. They joined the Union Army in search of freedom

Invisible Southerners

Georgia Southern University
Jack N. and Addie D. Averitt Lecture Series
Number 14

Invisible Southerners

Ethnicity in the Civil War

ANNE J. BAILEY

The University of Georgia Press

Athens and London

© 2006 by the University of Georgia Press

Athens, Georgia 30602

All rights reserved

Printed and bound by Maple-Vail

The paper in this book meets the guidelines for
permanence and durability of the Committee on
Production Guidelines for Book Longevity of the
Council on Library Resources.

Printed in the United States of America

10 09 08 07 06 c 5 4 3 2 1

Library of Congress Cataloging-in-Publication Data

Bailey, Anne J.

Invisible Southerners : ethnicity in the Civil War / Anne J. Bailey.

p. cm. — (Jack N. and Addie D. Averitt lecture series ; no. 14)

Includes bibliographical references and index.

ISBN-13: 978-0-8203-2757-0 (hardcover : alk. paper)

ISBN-10: 0-8203-2757-3 (hardcover : alk. paper)

1. United States—History—Civil War, 1861–1865—Participation, German American.

2. United States—History—Civil War, 1861–1865—Participation, Indian.

3. United States—History—Civil War, 1861–1865—Participation, African American.

4. German Americans—Southern States—History—19th century.

5. Indians of North America—Southern States—History—19th century.

6. African Americans—Southern States—History—19th century.

7. Confederate States of America—Social conditions. I. Title. II. Series.

E540.G3B35 2006

973.7′086′930975—dc22   2005020762

British Library Cataloging-in-Publication Data available

CONTENTS

FOREWORD

On October 4 and 5, 2004, the Department of History at Georgia Southern University hosted the fourteenth annual Jack N. and Addie D. Averitt Lecture Series. The speaker was Anne J. Bailey, professor of history at Georgia College & State University and editor of the *Georgia Historical Quarterly*. Professor Bailey's lectures addressed an often-overlooked aspect of the American Civil War—the nontraditional soldier. Bailey focused on men of ethnic backgrounds other than Anglo-American and specifically addressed the contributions of southern Native Americans, German Americans, and African Americans.

Professor Bailey opened the 2004 series with an examination of the dilemmas facing the indigenous peoples living within or on the boundaries of the newborn Confederacy. Several nations, the Cherokee being the largest, hesitated to jeopardize existing treaty arrangements with the United States (and all that those treaties represented in terms of entitlements), but were likewise reluctant to sacrifice the wealth and status associated with slavery—an institution that many, but not all, southern tribes adopted. Bailey detailed the political and military efforts of men such as Albert Pike, John Ross, and Stand Watie who strove to guide native peoples through the adversity of war. In the end, Bailey concluded, Native Americans could not win no matter which side they chose or how they performed on the battlefield.

For German Americans living in the South, the focus of Bailey's second lecture, the Civil War raised disconcerting questions within families and communities. Prior to the war, immigrants who chose to settle below the Mason-Dixon Line were required to accept the reality of slavery no matter what their personal convictions about the "peculiar institution" were. With the outbreak of war, however, German immigrants were faced with pressure from their American-born neighbors to demonstrate their loyalty one way or another. Using the Lone Star State to illustrate her point, Bailey revealed how for many German Texans the war meant split allegiances, antiforeign harassment, and futile attempts at neutrality. Unfortunately for these Germans, Bailey lamented, there was no conscientious objector status in the Confederacy.

In her final lecture, Bailey traced the story of African Americans in the South and the Confederate and Union debates over their utility as soldiers. While propositions for arming blacks were almost nonexistent in the Confederacy until it was faced with its own demise in the spring of 1865, Union proposals to do just that began in earnest with Abraham Lincoln's final Emancipation Proclamation in January 1863. Bailey outlined the consternation such ideas created within Confederate and Union ranks and detailed the opinion and reaction of one of the staunchest opponents to Lincoln's policy within the Union military—Major General William Tecumseh Sherman. Bailey concluded by highlighting the contributions and sacrifices of the African Americans who served in the United States Colored Troops from its inception to the end of the war.

All three of these lectures are presented here—albeit in a slightly different order. Without the worries of the time constraints inherent in a lecture format, Professor Bailey had the luxury of developing her ideas more fully in the preparation of this manuscript and including additional information to which her audiences at Georgia Southern were not privy.

Many people are to be thanked for their support and encouragement in making this lecture series possible. Foremost is Dr. Jack Averitt who, along with his late wife, Addie, established the series to enrich the academic and cultural life of Georgia Southern University and the community at large. Thanks to the Averitts' generosity, Dr. Bailey joins a distinguished group of previous speakers—Eugene D. Genovese, James Olney, George B. Tindall, Tony Tanner, Samuel S. Hill Jr., Barbara Hardy, Catherine Clinton, Houston A. Baker Jr., Betty Wood, Don Doyle, Russ McDonald, David Goldfield, and

Gerald Bruns—who have made the series such a success since its endowment in 1990.

The faculty and administration of Georgia Southern University have provided enthusiastic support for the Averitt Lectures since the inception of the series. Thanks go to University President Bruce Grube, Provost Linda Bleicken, Dean of the College of Liberal Arts and Social Sciences Jane Rhoades Hudak, and Department of History Chair Sandra Peacock who continue the long tradition of recognizing the importance of the series to the university and the community. Graduate students from the Department of History served as ushers during the lectures and performed a variety of duties throughout the two-day event. Nicole Mitchell of the University of Georgia Press offered helpful advice and assistance during the publication process. Dr. Anastatia Sims, my cochair on the Department of History's Averitt Lecture Series Committee, provided incomparable assistance as she worked diligently to keep me on track and to tackle the responsibilities necessary to make this year's series a success. Finally, a very sincere debt of gratitude goes to Lisa Sapp and Fran Aultman who put aside their normal duties as secretaries in the department to tackle the crucial task of promoting the lectures.

ALAN C. DOWNS
Cochair, Averitt Lecture Series Committee

The day that Professor Anastatia Sims invited me to present the Jack N. and Addie D. Averitt Lectures at Georgia Southern University in November 2004, I felt very honored, as I had taught at GSU early in my career and considered the Averitt Lectures as one of the most prestigious lecture series in America. I accepted at once, without even thinking about possible topics. Later I realized the responsibility I had accepted to produce something scholarly, something important, and something that I would feel comfortable discussing with authority but that would still center on a theme general enough to appeal to a diverse audience. After some thought I decided that I would focus on nontraditional Civil War soldiers, those men who are not always remembered as being Southern at the time of the American Civil War. I wanted to examine what it meant to be a Southern-born or Southern-raised male in the turbulent decades before the conflict and how men of military age from various ethnic groups reacted to the challenge when war came.

I had first come across nontraditional Southern soldiers while working on a sociomilitary history of a cavalry brigade during graduate school. By *nontraditional* I mean soldiers who were not white males with roots stretching back to the British Isles even though they were, by and large, Southern born and raised. In my research, I found Germans sprinkled throughout the companies, and one entire company composed of Native Americans. I had not expected to find this, for in my graduate-student days I believed the Confederate armies were filled with men of English, Scottish, Scotch-Irish, Irish, and Welsh ancestry.

Our image of a Rebel soldier can be seen today on almost every courthouse square in the South, for Southerners immortalized the men who went to war in the postwar years with impressive statues. In Milledgeville, the capital of Georgia during the Civil War, the Confederate soldier has been moved, as many were during the turbulent decade of the 1960s, and now sits alone and hidden by shrubs across the street from the public library. But he is typical: a striking white male holding his trusty musket, an image carved in stone, and a symbol of what was best in the South in 1861. The postwar Southerners who commissioned these statues intended to immortalize native-born white males; they did not intend to honor foreigners—and certainly not Native Americans. Today we visualize the Confederate soldier in a certain way, for it is the one that Hollywood has reinforced in cinema for the last nine decades. It is the one that emerged when Southerners espoused the Lost Cause in the years following defeat. In spite of the revisionist histories of recent years, our image of the Confederate soldier still resembles Margaret Mitchell's famous fictional character Ashley Wilkes. Men like Wilkes, who bore defeat with honor and dignity, came to symbolize the gallant cavalier of the defeated South.

But almost 140 years since the end of the Civil War, there are still stories that need telling in spite of the fact that the number of works published about the war each year remains high. Books on Robert E. Lee continue to sell, as such revered leaders will always have an audience. Battle studies remain popular. A keyword search for Gettysburg on *Amazon.com* brings up thousands of results. Yet battles in the Virginia theater, or even those in Tennessee, Mississippi, Alabama, and Georgia, do not tell the whole story.

For Southerners in 1861 the Confederate military was a white man's world inhabited by native-born Southerners. Few Southerners knew that three Confederate cabinet posts included men who were foreign born: Judah P. Benjamin, who served as attorney general, secretary of war, and secretary of state, was born on Saint Croix in the West Indies; Stephen Mallory, the secretary of the navy, was born in Trinidad; and Secretary of the Treasury Christopher Memminger was a native of Germany. Among the Confederacy's fighting men, Brigadier General William Browne was from England, Major General Patrick R. Cleburne was Irish born, and Major General Prince Camille Armand Jules Marie de Polignac was French. Polignac was the only foreigner to rise to major general, as Cleburne and Browne were naturalized citizens. Long before our modern political parties saw the importance of the Cuban vote in Florida, Cubans of Hispanic origin fought for both sides in the Civil War (one recent book surveys Cubans in the Confederacy). Clearly the rank and file of the Confederate army embraced a wide variety of ethnic groups, including Irish, German, English, French, Hispanic, and even a few of the most unexpected, Native American. The religions of these various ethnic groups—Protestantism, Roman Catholicism, Judaism, traditional tribal Indian beliefs—were as varied as the soldiers themselves.

As a people we create a collective memory; as Southerners we focus on what is most important to the South. Often that collective historical memory excludes what does not fit into the accepted stereotype. As a result, it was not unusual for various ethnic groups to be overlooked in the writings of postwar historians, and even early twentieth-century historians generally ignored their presence. The role of Native Americans has not received the attention it deserves, while battles such as Gettysburg receive more attention than might be necessary. And while studies involving Native Americans are increasing, it is difficult to separate fact from fiction. Questions surrounding Indian atrocities at the Battle of Pea Ridge, Arkansas, in 1862, still draw more attention than the legitimate contributions that Native Americans gave to the Confederate States of America. It is also difficult to integrate Native American history into the accepted lore of the Civil War. Southerners still prefer the land of cavaliers that Margaret Mitchell immortalized. They reject stories that involve tomahawks rather than muskets, scalpings instead of heroic deaths in battle. Only recently have revisionist views of the war become more common, with historians looking at women's roles, the guerrilla war, and the contributions of ethnic groups other than native-born white Anglo-Saxon and Celtic Southerners.

In the past academics overlooked the various ethnic groups with the same blindness present in the wider Southern culture. Civil War historians stayed away from the battles involving Native Americans generally for two reasons. First, most of the battles involving Indians were fought west of the Mississippi River in a region that does not interest readers nor researchers as much as the battles in the eastern theater of Virginia or the western theater of Georgia, Alabama, Mississippi, and Tennessee. Second, writing about Native Americans necessitates knowing their prewar history, for in some cases the war caused old divisions to reemerge more powerful than ever. At the same time, historians of Native Americans tend to avoid the war years except in passing, for to write a comprehensive history of military engagements one must learn commanders and departments, military politics both North and South, and strategy and tactics. In the past such things have not often interested a researcher in the social or cultural history of Native Americans. Military history was left to the military historian, while social and ethnic history became entirely different fields. Only recently have these subfields merged, and there is a growing number of works on the various ethnic groups in both the Southern and Northern armies. The new military history integrates various perspectives with social, economic, political, and cultural topics. Not only do modern authors discuss what happened, they explain why it mattered.

My choices for the three lectures—and thus for the three chapters of this book—therefore, devolved upon the questions of ethnicity and some of those ethnic groups most ignored in Civil War history. For the first chapter, I decided on the divided loyalties of German Americans, both those born in Europe and those born on American soil. The designation "German American" generally applied to a person who came, or whose immediate ancestors came, from a region in Europe where the prominent language was German and whose primary language spoken in the home continued to be German. Beyond that there was wide diversity. Many German-speaking Americans were Roman Catholic, some were Protestant, and even a few were Jewish. Attitudes toward slavery varied as much as the religions they held and the regions from which they had come. Slavery had long been illegal in Europe, but immigrants to the United States had to deal with the South's "peculiar institution." Many German immigrants never came to the South but settled in the North to avoid the controversy. Those who did move to the South had to learn to live alongside the institution even if they did not approve. When the war came, their loyalty to the Confederacy was brought into question.

For the second chapter, I chose Native Americans, for many tribes loyally supported the Confederacy. In writing such an account, it is necessary to establish some guidelines concerning the use of language. While "Native Americans" has become more common in modern society, the use of the word "Indian" is prevalent in nineteenth-century sources. I have used the words interchangeably as synonyms, and indeed, that may become more common with the opening of the Smithsonian Institution's National Museum of the American Indian in Washington, D.C., in 2004. Tribal designations are also difficult. I have chosen to use a plural noun in all references to tribes as groups (e.g., Creeks). Another problem is the use of the word "civilize" where it is used as a label to describe certain "civilized tribes." Such descriptions portray Native Americans from a superior white point of view and assume that tribes were uncivilized if they had not become Christian or had failed to adopt white ways. To discuss the tribes that participated in the Civil War is impossible, however, without using the language that was current at the time, and I have followed those conventions.

The final chapter—on African Americans—was the hardest of the three. Although African Americans were native-born Southerners, many black men of military age elected to support the Union when the promise of freedom was presented. They were truly the most invisible Southerners in the Civil War, for they were persecuted for the choice they made, both by the Northern soldiers they fought with and by the white Rebel soldiers who punished them if they were captured. They fought for freedom in a slave society, and decades, almost a century in fact, would pass before their contribution received any widespread recognition. One important point to consider is how these men are identified in modern books. Although the use of African American is generally accepted in today's society, the soldiers are typically referred to as black. Therefore I have used both terms.

Clearly I could not look at all the ethnic groups in the South that participated in the war. The Irish, for example, were the largest ethnic group in the United States. But unlike the Germans, the Irish spoke English, had ties to their British Isles roots, and were not generally singled out, except in their religious practices. Some ethnic groups made a limited contribution to the war effort, Native Americans, for example, while others, such as African Americans, made a fairly significant contribution, at least numerically, although it was on the Northern side. The brief analyses that follow are only a sample of the growing literature on this important topic.

I would also like to take this opportunity to express my gratitude to Dr. Jack Averitt for his generosity in endowing this lecture series. I enjoyed seeing old friends while in Statesboro, particularly Frank Saunders, Don Rakestraw, James and Becky Woods, Charlton and Jane Moseley, Peggy Hargis, George Shriver, and of course, the members of the committee, Anastatia Sims and Alan C. Downs, and his lovely wife Judi.

CHAPTER ONE

Broken Promises

German Immigrants and the Burden of America's Civil War

Foreigners came to America for many reasons, including freedom, but the promise of land and wealth was always one of the strongest attractions. In the three decades prior to the outbreak of the Civil War, nearly five million foreigners arrived in the United States. Most settled in the North—thus one out of every six persons living in free states by 1860 was foreign born. By contrast, only one in thirty individuals living in the Confederacy could claim a foreign birth. The population in 1860 of what would become the Confederate States was slightly more than nine million, but after subtracting free blacks and slaves, that left a white population of around five and a half million. Of these, about a quarter million had not been born on the American continent.

In colonial days Great Britain, France, and Spain had the greatest influence on religious and cultural values in the American South. These European powers eventually absorbed or destroyed centuries-old traditions practiced by indigenous Native Americans and immigrant Africans. Still, the land and climate forced immigrants to adopt new lifestyles, with the result that subregions developed in the new environment. For example, subcultures such as Creoles and Cajuns emerged in southern Louisiana. The blending of races in the Louisiana bayous is not surprising, however, for New Orleans counted the largest foreign population among cities in the South. Similarly, Louisiana led Southern states in the presence of foreign born, with foreigners making up more than 11 percent of its population by 1860.

The second largest number of foreigners could be found in Texas, where more than 7 percent of the population was foreign born. Texas was atypical of the land of cavaliers that became the mythic South of the popular imagination, but it was more typically Southern — as understood by nineteenth-century Southerners — than southern Louisiana. The large number of foreigners in New Orleans made that city more continental in the European style than traditionally Southern. Although Texas had a significant number of individuals who claimed Mexican birth and was the home of the second largest German American population in the American South, the majority of the state's residents had roots in one of the slave states. Southern culture and Southern traditions dominated. Anglo Texans restricted the influence of Mexican Americans to south Texas, while German Texans tended to congregate in isolated communities.[1]

German-speaking Europeans who made America their home in the three decades before the Civil War left a continent that Napoleon Bonaparte had severely strained by years of conflict. Although peace came with his surrender in 1815, there was no longer a dominant Germanic power, and the German-speaking countries became a confederacy of independent states. Not until 1871, with the emergence of Imperial Germany, did a strong and unified nation appear, with the Prussian king as emperor. Therefore, between 1815 and 1871 people left for a variety of reasons, but religious freedom was not usually the primary cause as in the past. In the eighteenth century Salzburgers had settled in Georgia, Swiss Germans had emigrated to Purrysburg in South Carolina, and Moravians had moved to North Carolina. But many of these communities, often religious in nature, had failed to survive. As a result, Germans had difficulty imposing their cultural values on any particular region. By the 1840s many Germans began to arrive at the port of New Orleans, and they moved up the Mississippi River in search of a place to make a new life. By the 1850s the foreign population of Memphis and Louisville had grown by as much as 10 or 15 percent. Richmond also attracted Germans seeking work in the city's iron industry. By the time of the Civil War some fifty-three thousand Germans lived in Texas, Louisiana, and Virginia, with more than half, or thirty thousand, in the Lone Star State.[2]

One researcher recently surveyed published works containing Civil War diaries or collections of letters written by German-speaking participants in the nation's great conflict. He looked at those originally composed in German but published in English; only ten have come to light. Seven were written by Germans in the Union army. The other three, all Confederate, were written by Germans in Texas. Even journal articles on the subject are scarce. Certainly those letters and diaries penned in German had little attraction for the children and grandchildren of the immigrants, whose native tongue in the succeeding generations was English, and even less attraction for modern researchers who do not read German. Moreover, at the beginning of the twentieth century, the anti-German bias reached great height when the United States joined the fighting in World War I. Twenty years later World War II brought another wave of anti-German sentiment. Both world wars destroyed most German folkways in America and prohibited the use of the German language. Many families probably threw away documents in German hoping to become more "American"; certainly, emphasizing one's German heritage was not fashionable. Not until the 1960s, with the building of the Berlin Wall and President John F. Kennedy's promise to protect and defend West Berlin in the face of Soviet aggression during the Cold War, did it become generally acceptable to study German Americans. By then, for all practical purposes, Germans had assimilated into Southern culture, many even having changed their names to avoid discrimination, and much of what is needed to research Germans in the antebellum South had been lost or destroyed. What German influence remains in the South today is generally the result of modern tourism. An excellent example of this is Helen in north Georgia, a town transformed into a Bavarian village in the 1970s and currently the third most frequently visited site in Georgia behind Atlanta and Savannah.[3]

One common myth regarding the Old South is that "southern ways were English ways." Today we understand that the Old South was a mix of many cultures, not just English, Irish, Scotch-Irish, Welsh, and Scottish. If Europe was a blend of Old World ways and culture, the South was even more so in the early days, but by the nineteenth century much of the cultural diversity came from within. Outsiders often preferred to immigrate to the North. The colonial South had developed some peculiar traits, the most obvious being the continued presence of slaves, and immigrants to the antebellum South had to accept a society based on bondage. This was not always easy for Europeans. German-speaking Europeans often stood out because they retained their own language, music, and cuisine. Northerner Frederick Law Olmsted, who visited the South in the 1850s, said he was much more comfortable in German homes, for the "neat houses and diligent merchants, mechanics, and farmers reminded him of New England." Perhaps even more telling was that Olmsted praised Germans for serving vegetables and wheat bread to guests and complained that native-born Southerners preferred to offer visitors greasy "bacon and corn pone."[4]

By the 1830s German immigration to the South focused mainly on Texas. A group of noblemen had visions of settling German peasants in the American Southwest and in the advertisements Texas was described as a "land with a winterless climate like that of Sicily." The land was fertile, and fish and game were abundant. All the land needed was hardworking Germans to make it productive. So even before Texas joined the United States, it had attracted the attention of foreigners. The German entrepreneurs who wanted to establish a Germanic foothold in the Southwest brought settlers whose traditions and values differed from the people who came from the American South. On arriving in their new home, however, Germans learned quickly that the brochures had left out some important points, such as the presence of unfriendly Comanches and Kiowas. Nobody had mentioned half-inch hail or vicious thunderstorms that leveled crops either. And as soon as families from the American South joined the immigration to Texas, the Europeans had to assimilate or remain silent on the institution of slavery. This seemed to work until the secession crisis forced them to declare their support for the South's peculiar institution or break the law. There was no room for moral objections in the Confederate States of America.[5]

That does not mean that Germans as a whole embraced or rejected the Confederacy. Germans in Louisville, Kentucky, enlisted in Union units, while Germans in Wilmington, North Carolina, enthusiastically joined a local Confederate regiment. The German Volunteers formed in Charleston, South Carolina, and South Carolina Germans soon organized other companies. Regiments from Louisiana, Virginia, Tennessee, and Georgia all enrolled loyal German Americans. Although in Texas the majority of Germans had arrived only in the two decades preceding the Civil War, the Lone Star State still saw a significant number of Germans become Confederate soldiers. At the same time, Texas was the only state where German communities divided over the meaning of patriotism.

More than 30,000 Germans lived in a state with a free population of slightly more than 421,000. In 1860, four of the state's largest cities, Galveston, Houston, San Antonio, and New Braunfels, were located in predominantly German counties. The Germans had not spread throughout the settled regions; the majority had congregated in south-central Texas, on a line running from the coastal plain around Houston to the Hill Country outside of San Antonio and Austin. By living in confined communities, they had managed to retain their European lifestyle, language, and cultural values. This German belt was the result of a process known as "chain migration." One individual or a group of individuals migrated, and others soon followed. The first German to come to Texas, Johann Friedrich Ernst, arrived in 1831. He wrote letters home that persuaded other Germans to follow. This device, known as the "American letter," is studied by students of migration. Such letters accounted for much of the migration in the antebellum period; they stressed the positive and downplayed the negative. In short, advertisements claimed America was a paradise on earth.[6]

Why these Germans came to America is debatable. Some historians believe that they were simply lured by the promise of free land and that politics played little or no part in their exodus from Europe.

Although this may be true, the German settlers do seem to fall into two categories—those who came before the European revolutions of 1848 and those who came after. People called the early arrivals the "grays," while the "greens," or "Forty-eighters," had come in the 1850s. Some historians argue that the grays were basically conservative while the greens were more liberal and intellectual. Others do not believe that there was any significant political difference. No matter, the number of Germans in the state was significant.[7]

Texas Germans congregated in rural towns where they could maintain a traditional lifestyle without competition from outside influences. By isolating their communities they could avoid trouble with anti-immigrant political groups like the Know-Nothings and evade the notice of antiforeign Southerners. To prosper and become part of the larger community, Germans generally accepted the existing state government and some even became proponents of the institution of slavery and states' rights. A few even purchased slaves. Yet an equal number silently objected to slavery. Frederick Law Olmsted, who visited Texas in 1854, observed that few Germans concerned "themselves with the theoretical right or wrong of the institution" and, when it did not "interfere with their own liberty or progress," were "careless of its existence." In any case, some antislavery Germans became abolitionist in thought if not in practice. After the election of Abraham Lincoln in November 1860 and the secession of South Carolina in December, Germans had to take a stand on the South's peculiar institution.[8]

Although slavery was an important issue, Germans had practical reasons to support or reject the Confederate States of America when secessionists established the new government in Montgomery, Alabama, in January 1861. The earliest arrivals had founded towns on land purchased by developers; the later arrivals ended up moving further west, eventually settling on the frontier where Kiowas and Comanches still threatened daily existence. The U.S. Army had established a line of forts to protect the scattered towns and farms. It was along this line of forts, from the mid-1850s until 1861, that Robert E. Lee served as lieutenant colonel of the Second U.S. Cavalry. With the secession crisis came the very practical concern about what would happen if the army departed. As a result, Germans leaned toward rejecting secession based on the very real need to keep the federal army in place rather than any concern over the institution of slavery.[9]

Although Texas was the only state with an active Indian frontier, it was still basically Southern. Most of the population had come from the slave states or those free states bordering on the Ohio River—Indiana, Illinois, and Ohio—where attitudes toward blacks, both slave and free, resembled those of residents in the slaveholding states south of the river. The modern concept of Texas as western rather than Southern is a relatively modern invention. In the Texas Centennial Exposition in 1936, promoters who wanted to break the link with what was then considered the "backward, slaveholding, agrarian South" of the Great Depression advertised the state as part of the West. They used chorus girls in chaps and ten-gallon hats to promote the new image. A Texas Ranger, on a horse named Texas, galloped into hotel lobbies armed with two .45-caliber six-shooters. With such publicity, the state's link to the Old South faded and the mythology of Texas as cowboy country, with productive oil fields as a bonus, began. The 1956 movie version of Edna Ferber's best-selling novel *Giant* solidified the image, and the success of the television series *Dallas*, which ran from 1978 until 1991, broke any remaining links to the Old South, for J. R. Ewing was a ruthless Texas oilman who lived on the cattle ranch of Southfork. But the Texas of the twentieth century was not the Texas of 1861, and that mistake often leads to a misunderstanding of the state's history. The German immigrants who came to Texas in the decades before the Civil War came to a state that closely resembled Georgia, Alabama, Mississippi, or Tennessee. Plantations dotted the Gulf Coast. When the war came, Texans voted exactly as one would expect of immigrants from slaveholding states. Even those who came from the Midwest often supported secession, and only small pockets of resistance surfaced among Northern-born immigrants.[10]

What is known about Germans in the Confederate army is fragmented. Ella Lonn published her classic study *Foreigners in the Confederacy* in 1940, just after the outbreak of World War II, and most readers accepted her stereotypes at a time when Germany's aggressive war in Europe stirred antiforeign sentiment in America. Lonn, who had been born in 1879, was herself the daughter of a Swedish immigrant. Although she discussed all foreigners in the Confederacy, she estimated that around 72,000 Germans lived in the South as compared with 1.3 million in the North. But the records are scarce, so she had to base her estimates on the 1860 federal census. The Irish, of course, were the most numerous, while those who had immigrated from Germany came in second. Native-born Southerners primarily composed the Confederate armies, and foreigners were not welcome unless they had adopted Southern ways. For example, a Virginian, who noted the ethnic makeup of the Confederate army, did so by observing the effect alcohol had on each nationality: Whiskey, he concluded, "induces a Frenchman to talk, and he shines out, the very embodiment of the graces." An Englishman, he judged, "grows affectionate." On the Irish, liquor had a boisterous effect: "Four fingers of stone-fence whiskey will set an Irishman fighting as surely as St. Patrick was a gentleman." Finally, he concluded, Germans had more trouble assimilating because a German who drinks too much "becomes gloomy and morose." These stereotypes had their roots in Old World prejudices and would continue into the twentieth century.[11]

Much more research has been done on the ethnic makeup of Union armies. In 1951 Lonn published her last book, *Foreigners in the Union Army and Navy*, and thirty-seven years later, in 1988, William C. Burton's *Melting Pot Soldiers: The Union's Ethnic Regiments* updated her groundbreaking work. Lonn, whose work on Unionist Germans appeared only six years after Hitler's defeat, reinforced the stereotype that Germans made good soldiers, as they were "industrious and thrifty" and "well disciplined, persevering, and inspired by some idealism." Moreover, she added, Germans "were somewhat slow in response but were stable and solid in battle; they learned, in fact, to do some skillful fighting. Leisurely in their mental processes, they had a passion for thoroughness in the details of warfare as in everything." She could have easily been writing about Adolf Hitler's soldiers. A recent critic of Lonn, historian Earl Hess, has noted that she stressed tired stereotypes and relied "too heavily on obscure German language publications, written by German-Americans, adulatory of the Germans who fought in the Civil War." Not coincidentally, the time in which she was writing was also soon after that in which the German general Erwin Rommel had become the legendary "Desert Fox" of the World War II North African campaigns.

Still, because of the large number of German immigrants in the North, Germans sometimes composed complete regiments, a regiment comprising one thousand to twelve hundred or more men. New York had ten regiments consisting almost entirely of Germans; the Union XI Corps had twenty-six regiments, fifteen almost totally German. Therefore, in the North the strong racism against Germans was often acted out in the camps. American-born soldiers thought the Germans "dumb Dutchmen" and would often laugh at units as they marched by, remarking in a derisive manner, "The air around here is rather Dutchy!"[12]

Stereotypes prevailed in antebellum America, and the Know-Nothing Party had encouraged bigotry and racism. Feelings against Germans prevailed in both armies. A Massachusetts soldier thought of Germans as the "lower order" and wrote: "Fresh meat was issued. After we had removed every particle of meat from the bones, General Blenker's corps, who were in camp near us, took the leavings, such as bones, entrails, etcs., and had a regular Thanksgiving dinner on what our luxurious natures discarded as useless."[13]

The eminent historian Bell Irvin Wiley, whose classic, *The Life of Johnny Reb*, first appeared in 1943, in the middle of World War II, had an entire chapter devoted to the kind of men who fought for the South but only made brief and vague references to Germans. He noted, "Their love for music enlivened the atmosphere of many encampments, and when convinced of the rightness of the Confederate cause, as they doubtless were in a majority of cases, they acquitted themselves creditably on the firing line." Yet of the German Texans, he concluded, they "were notoriously unsympathetic toward the Southern cause," although he added, almost in contradiction, that "many served faithfully and gallantly."[14]

Cultural geographer Terry Jordan reminds us that Germans who settled in the South were a diverse lot. There were peasant farmers as well as intellectuals; there were Protestants, Catholics, Jews, and atheists; frugal and honest folk emigrated to the South alongside the occasional ax murderer. There were "stern, teetotaling German Methodists, who renounced dancing and fraternal organizations," as well as "fun-loving, hardworking Lutherans and Catholics who enjoyed drinking and dancing." There were also Germans who were descended from "intellectual political refugees" and who scorned the need for religion of any sort. And yet, even with such diverse religious and cultural characteristics, the German settlers' distinctive customs, language, architecture, and foods set them apart from native-born Southerners. They enjoyed spiced sausage and sauerkraut and drank German beer. They polkaed in the dance halls and enjoyed German pastimes. "In the neighborhood of San Antonio, one-third of the population is German," observed Colonel Arthur Fremantle, an Englishman who passed through Texas in the spring of 1863. "The houses are well built of stone," he added, and Menger's hotel, owned by a German, was a "large and imposing edifice." Frederick Law Olmsted had also noted the varied ethnic groups in the heart of the city when he wrote, "The sauntering Mexicans prevail on the pavements, but the bearded Germans and the sallow Yankees furnish their proportion."[15]

Germans in the South had more problems than just antiforeign bias. In the South a person had to support the Confederacy or face the condemnation of neighbors. In Kentucky, for example, some twenty-seven thousand Germans supported the Union, but only two thousand actually served in the Union army. Possibly, those who enlisted in the Union army were veterans of the revolutions of 1848. Somewhere between four and ten thousand of those individuals came to the United States, and they became the more radical elements of the immigrant population. The Forty-eighters tended to be enemies of the Catholic Church, often even atheists, and these political refugees frequently became abolitionists. Although some 960,000 Germans came to the United States in the 1850s, this small radical element became the one that Americans—including Southerners—associated with the foreign born in their communities. But most Germans were not radical. In fact, many came from the southern regions of Germany and were Roman Catholic. Some German immigrants simply saw the rebellion of 1861 as a threat to political stability and much too close to what had happened in their own country in 1848. One German who joined the Eighth Missouri (Union) observed that he "grasped the weapon of death for the purpose of doing [his] part in defending and upholding the integrity, laws, and the preservation of [his] adopted country from a band of contemptible traitors who would if they [could] accomplish their hellish designs, destroy the best and noblest government on earth."[16]

Although a number of Germans had strong feelings about secession, generally based on their own personal needs, the majority remained neutral. In Texas, a few pro-Union German newspaper editors pointed out the necessity of protecting the settlements from hostile Indians and argued that the U.S. government, having had that chore since the end of the Mexican War, was much better able to do so than the proposed Southern nation. American-born Texans probably gave little thought to the Germans who had settled in their midst prior to the secession crisis, but as soon as outspoken German editors took a stand against secession, the isolated towns became the focus of suspicion and distrust.[17]

Although the Texas Secession Convention voted 166 to 8 to leave the Union, the delegates called for a general election to approve the decision. To reach all the voters, the delegates had ten thousand copies of the document printed in English, two thousand in Spanish, and another two thousand in German. In the general election in February, 76 percent supported secession, while only 24 percent voiced their opposition. The regions opposed tended to be located in north Texas along the Red River and in the German counties of central Texas. But even within these regions, there were inconsistencies. Comal County, in the center of the German settlements, voted 239 to 86 in favor of secession, while Gillespie County, on the Indian frontier, voted 398 to 16 against. Although this may have more to do with the fact that frontier settlers did not want the U.S. Army to evacuate the posts protecting them from the hostile Plains Indians, a significant number of German Texans obviously still felt some loyalty to the U.S. government.[18]

Most German Texans avoided controversial topics, particularly their personal beliefs about slavery and states' rights, until the state seceded. But after the Confederate Congress passed a banishment act on August 8, 1861, which required all males over fourteen years of age who were considered hostile to the Confederate government to leave within forty days, they had to take a stand. The law allowed state officials to arrest, remove, or confine aliens "against whom complaints may be made" by district attorneys, marshals, and other Confederate officers. In a presidential proclamation in mid-August, Jefferson Davis declared that any foreigners who did not declare their loyalty to the Confederacy and remained in the South after the grace period expired would be treated as alien enemies. German Texans, therefore, either voiced their allegiance to the Confederacy or feigned support. A few, mainly those in the settlements nestled in the Texas Hill Country, passively resisted. The only other alternative — to depart the state within forty days — meant they would lose everything they had worked for since arriving in America.[19]

Although the budding disaffection did not go unnoticed, it was not a major concern of the state government until the spring of 1862, when the passage of the conscription act forced foreigners to declare their loyalties. State officials already knew there was resentment within the alien population, for some agents of the Confederate government had suffered harassment in several predominantly German counties early in the year. But the resistance, typically unorganized, was localized and did not pose a serious threat to the state government. Many men of foreign birth voiced legal objections based on the grounds that an alien owed no military service to the Confederacy. The Confederate government generally avoided dealing with the complicated question by requiring home defense, rather than regular military service, from most foreigners. In Texas, however, Governor Francis R. Lubbock, a staunch secessionist who had won office in a heated election in August 1861, believed that any foreigner who refused to serve should be required to leave the state. Tension increased as Germans fled, some heading for Unionist communities-in-exile in Mexico.

At the same time, the state government kept a close eye on the activities of known Unionists. One individual the state closely monitored was Andrew Jackson Hamilton, a former Austin attorney, acting attorney general, and member of the U.S. Congress. He was also a political ally of Sam Houston and during 1861 had worked to find a compromise that would avoid conflict. When this failed, Hamilton resumed his Unionist activities, and the Alabama-born Hamilton soon won the support of German Unionists. Brigadier General Hamilton P. Bee, who commanded the Sub-Military District of the Rio Grande, reported, "Information was received establishing the fact that Jack Hamilton and other traitors were unquestionably in arms against the Government and had assembled in the counties designated, their force being variously estimated at from 100 to 500." Bee also claimed that he had evidence that the "traitors were moving their goods and families, with large supplies of provisions, into the mountain districts, and were carrying off the property in some instances of loyal citizens, and at last, to set beyond a doubt their objects and intentions, positive intelligence was received of their having waylaid and murdered one or two well-known secession or loyal citizens." Hamilton fled to Mexico with a small band of supporters in the spring of 1862, leaving behind growing concern about the loyalty of settlers in south-central Texas. In particular, his activities focused the state's attention on Unionist activities in central Texas.[20]

To avoid being singled out, many Germans declared their loyalty to the Confederacy on paper while remaining neutral in thought and action. This seemed to work, rather like the modern military policy of "don't ask, don't tell." Nonetheless, German efforts to recruit companies for home defense could cause problems. When a group known as the Union Loyal League organized in Gillespie, Kerr, and Kendall counties, the members had to disavow any seditious motives. They claimed their only agenda was to protect civilians from hostile Indians and roving bands of guerrillas and maintained their intentions were "to prevent strife between Union and Confederate partisans; to take such peaceable action as would prevent the forced enlistment of Union sympathizers in the Confederate army; and to protect the homes and families within the area embraced in the limits of the 'Union Loyal League' against marauding bands of Indians." Unconvinced, Confederate general Bee blamed some of the troubles in the state on men who were "chiefly foreigners by birth" and who seemed "greatly disaffected and were organizing and arming to resist the law known as the conscript act." As concern grew, state officials ordered Confederate cavalry composed of American-born troopers to the town of Fredericksburg in the Texas Hill Country. Fredericksburg is known today as a quaint tourist town, the birthplace of Chester Nimitz, commander of U.S. naval forces in the Pacific Ocean during World War II. But in 1862 it was a small settlement on the Indian frontier, the seat of Gillespie County, and a center of Union sentiment.[21]

After General Bee declared martial law in April, he required citizens to take an oath of allegiance to the state of Texas and the Confederate nation, arresting anyone who refused. He also established camps of conscription, and soldiers assigned to these camps were "to hunt out persons liable to military duty that did not volunteer, and send them into some regiment." The Confederate commander found the residents "shy and timid" and observed that the few locals "who were friendly to the Government did not possess moral courage enough to give information to the provost-marshal of the sayings and doings of those who [were] unfriendly."[22]

When opposition to conscription spread throughout the region, Brigadier General Paul O. Hébert, in command of the Military District of Texas and Louisiana, extended martial law statewide and specifically told German Unionists that they were expected to comply. His declaration appeared in both English and German in local newspapers. Anyone who failed to appear before the provost marshal had to pay a five-dollar fine, and a German paper in New Braunfels warned that men of military age who refused to comply would be "vigorously dealt with." The English visitor Arthur Fremantle noted that the Germans in San Antonio "objected much to the conscription, and some even resisted by force of arms."[23]

Draft evaders troubled the Confederate government in every state, but in Texas the problem was complex. Men who did not want to serve in the military could disappear along the Indian frontier, particularly in the Texas Hill Country. Central Texas, the site of the later German settlements, contained the oldest and most folded rocks in the state. The Balcones Fault zone curved northeast from San Antonio through Austin and Georgetown and beyond. Much like the Fall Line in Georgia divides the state, the Balcones Fault divided the older and harder rocks to the northwest from the younger and more easily eroded rocks to the south and east. The harder rocks to the west form hills rising noticeably above the softer rocks to the east, a topographic expression that caused the early Spaniards to call it "Los Balcones" or "the balconies."

During various geologic eras the landscape had eroded in ways that had created some of the most fascinating landscape in the state. For example, the town of Fredericksburg is on land eroded by the Pedernales River. The higher hills to the north dominate most of the skyline in the area. In fact, the landscape in central Texas includes a vast array of features: coarse-grained pink granite and gneiss hills, outcroppings of pure granite covered with brush and trees, and prairies covered with shrubs.

This was the landscape that many German settlers faced. When the later settlers arrived in Texas, the fertile flat land had long fallen into the hands of American-born Southern planters and farmers, and the newcomers encountered a more challenging and hostile environment. Obviously, large plantations were impossible, but the Germans generally preferred small farms anyway, as they had no tradition that involved cotton and slaves. The main problem, however, was that the hills provided cover for raiding Indian parties. And during the war the hills also became the perfect place for draft evaders to hide.

As a result, Confederate soldiers patrolled the hills around Fredericksburg during the late spring and early summer of 1862. Following the passage of the conscription act state officials targeted foreigners, and Germans topped the list. Families of men suspected of evading the draft were rounded up and brought into town by parties of Confederate soldiers. "It was a pitiable sight to see all these poor folks stripped of their property, such as it was, earned by hard toil and exposure on a dangerous frontier," noted a sympathetic Texan. To prevent the persecution of their families and avoid conscription, dissenters fled to Mexico, where Texas Unionists founded a small community in Matamoras, across the Rio Grande from Brownsville.[24]

State officials could hardly overlook such actions. Although other Confederate states struggled with Unionists, the problems generally centered on nonslaveholders living in such rugged mountain regions as northeast Georgia, east Tennessee, and western Virginia. In Texas the focus fell on the immigrant population. After rumors that German bushwhackers had attacked Confederate soldiers, authorities began prosecuting cases involving men arrested for violating martial law. After the murder of a farmer, state authorities declared Gillespie, Kendall, and Kerr counties in open rebellion, and around four hundred mounted Confederates headed to Gillespie County. A trooper described Fredericksburg as a village of some eight hundred people, "almost all of them Germans, and Unionists to a man."[25]

Violence between Confederates and Unionists seemed inevitable. In July a San Antonio newspaper claimed that the bones of Germans were "bleaching on the soil of every county from Red River to the Rio Grande and in the counties of Wise and Denton [in north Texas] their bodies [were] suspended by scores from the 'Black Jacks.'" Vigilante parties composed of Southern sympathizers hunted Unionists, and a Confederate soldier wrote in his diary on August 5 that scouts from his unit "found a man hanging right over the trail with his throat cut from ear to ear."[26]

Just a month before, several hundred people from central Texas had gathered near Fredericksburg, where some of the men decided to flee across the Rio Grande, and on August 1, some eighty men met west of Kerrville; sixty-one actually left for Mexico. State authorities could not dismiss such an obvious defiance of the law, and Confederate soldiers intercepted the Germans on the ninth at the Nueces River in Kinney County. The battle of the Nueces the following day ended with more than twenty Germans dead or wounded; the Confederates lost only two, with fewer than twenty wounded. There was no report of prisoners. A Confederate who had not actually been present noted, "A number of prisoners were taken; but all got away, so the boys said; and I know they would not lie about a little thing like that." In truth, more than thirty Germans escaped, although six were killed by Confederate troops in October while trying again to cross the Rio Grande, but most were apparently slaughtered on the spot and their bodies left unburied. "I cannot give that report any credence though," a Confederate German wrote his father, "because the man said, after the fight was over, the soldiers dragged the wounded away from the camping ground and had them shot dead one by one, and that seems very improbable to me." Still, for Germans living in the Hill Country, the incident became known as the "Nueces Massacre."[27]

After this episode tension increased in the German communities. A Confederate trooper observed: "There is now a daily guard around Fredericksburg. The 'bushwhackers' or traitors are plentiful in this country but keep themselves hid, and they have selected a good [hilly] country for the business. When *one* chances to fall into the hands of the C.S. soldiers he is dealt pretty roughly with and generally makes his last speech with a rope around his neck. Hanging is getting to be as common as hunting." Another soldier wrote in his diary: "We are having tough times in this neck of the woods these times. I counted seven men hung on one limb; cut down and thrown over the bluff into Spring Creek."[28]

As so often happens in civil wars the violence turned savage and lost that element of humanity that distinguishes so-called civilized wars from primitive conflicts. A Confederate soldier noted on August 27, "The *creeks* in this vicinity are said to be full of dead men!" He added that he "witnessed yesterday a sight which [he] never wish[ed] again to see in a civilized & enlightened country. In a water hole in Spring Creek (about 2 miles from camp) there are 4 *human bodies* lying on top of the water, thrown in and left to rot, and that too after they were hanged by neck and dead." He believed that dissenters should be prosecuted but observed, "If they are traitors no doubt they deserved their reward," but the Rebel soldiers "should have at least gave them a burial."[29]

In an effort to stem the violence, a change in policy occurred when Major General John Bankhead Magruder took charge of the department in late 1862; he encouraged moderation in dealing with the foreign settlements. He wanted immigrants who had been forced into the army removed from the state and warned his enrolling officers that this needed to be "done quietly and without show if such a thing be practicable, in order that all odious distinctions between the good and loyal citizens of foreign birth and those who are refractory may be obviated, and that no difficulties from this cause also may arise between . . . native-born citizens and those of foreign birth."[30]

Unfortunately for Magruder, he could not curb the rising tide of disaffection. A new center of discontent emerged in several settlements located in Colorado, Fayette, and Austin counties, the region directly west of Houston. Because these counties were far from the Hill Country and the towns lay on a line between Houston and Austin, Magruder visited the area personally. By February he could assure the governor "that a better state of feeling" existed in the "disaffected regions." Martial law did not extend beyond these three counties, and he hoped "soon to see the normal tribunals again in operation. The ringleaders, who had been apprehended, were by order turned over to the civil authorities, as these acts were committed prior to my declaration of martial law."[31]

Although it seemed to authorities that most Germans opposed the Confederacy, significant numbers of German Texans supported the South and joined Southern armies. Charles A. Leuschner, came to Texas from Prussia just before his tenth birthday. The family settled in Victoria, on the coast, and when the war came, he enlisted in the Sixth Texas Infantry Regiment. He had not celebrated his sixteenth birthday when he joined the army and was barely out of his teens when the war ended. Still, he was considered by his fellow soldiers "as one of the bravest, if not the bravest, of the brave." Another German Texan, Julius Giesecke, born in Hanover, Germany, in 1838, became the captain of a company from Washington County, northwest of Houston. Having arrived in the Lone Star State as a boy of seven, he had apparently assimilated into Southern culture with ease, and he remained intensely patriotic to the Confederacy to the end. Such was not always the case with his soldiers. "A great deal of dissatisfaction has arisen among the men, and several corporals in the company said that they wanted to resign," he wrote in March 1864. Although this incident "came to nothing," almost exactly one year later he complained, "Our regiment revolted and 127 men went home without leave of absence." Eighteen of the deserters came from his company of Germans. By the spring of 1865, however, many Confederates of Southern birth were also deserting, so too much should not be read into the deserters' ethnicities.[32]

Likewise, the Coreth family from New Braunfels sent three sons to the Confederate army. Unlike frontier settlements, such as Fredericksburg, New Braunfels, located between Austin and San Antonio, had a fairly large population and a stable economy that encouraged acceptance of the prevailing Southern culture. Although Northern traveler Frederick Olmsted had noted that New Braunfels had around three thousand Germans but just twenty Anglo-Americans, assimilation seemed more evident here than in the frontier regions, where the Indian problem concerned the immigrant population. Not many residents had voted in the national election of 1860, but those who did had voted Democratic. Only 86 of 325 men or 26 percent of Comal County voters had opposed secession.[33]

The county sent two companies of cavalry and one of infantry to the Confederate army, and throughout the war the local newspaper remained conservative, publishing articles supporting secession and states' rights. The first Coreth to enlist was twenty-three-year-old Rudolf, even though he could barely speak English and had met few people outside of the closed community. In November 1861, a month after he and a friend joined, he told his family back home: "We are treated as well here as we could possibly wish. The company consists almost entirely of Americans; we are the only Germans here."[34]

Although non-English speaking soldiers often suffered discrimination from their American-born comrades, there was also discrimination within the various ethnic groups. Many German-speaking soldiers retained Old World prejudices regarding other German-speaking soldiers from different regions of Europe. For example, Rudolf Coreth described a company he saw composed primarily of what he considered lower-class Germans and noted, "They behaved quite crudely all along the way" and, "in a word, [acted] like a real bunch of German yokels." When a German-speaking recruit joined his own company in February 1862, Rudolf Coreth again revealed his prejudices when he wrote, "I think he is a Silesian, [and] a boor." He added that he and his friend "would have been just as happy to be the only Germans in the company. But the others know the man and seem to like him quite well, and then we don't pay him much attention so that we won't be held responsible for his actions, and so I don't think he will detract from our status here much."[35]

Not until after the passage of the conscription act did Rudolf's two brothers enlist. Carl was twenty-five and Johann was nearly eighteen. The seeds of disaffection for the Confederacy could be seen when Rudolf failed to receive permission to transfer to the company his two siblings joined. He told his brother that he and his friend "positively" decided to reenlist only if they were allowed to fight alongside Carl and Johann. "If they do not want to give us any opportunity to do that," he continued, "they can defend their cause without us." The emphasis had become "they" and "their cause," not "us" and "our cause."[36]

Although the majority of German Texans who enlisted became loyal Confederate soldiers for the duration of the war, such was not the case for everyone. The Coreth family supported the Confederacy until Johann died in service in the summer of 1863. Although Rudolf had received permission to take his ill younger brother home, Johann did not survive the journey, and he was buried in an unmarked grave on the King Ranch in south Texas. As a result, the loyalty of Ernst Coreth, a father who had previously supported his sons' decision to join, declined. When local Germans held meetings to demonstrate their loyalty to the South, Ernst Coreth expressed his disgust with the growing inclination to feign support for the Confederacy in the German communities: "In San Antonio a War Meeting Barbecue in the grandest style has been announced for this coming Saturday. So naturally there is also a War Meeting in Podunk [*Krehwinkel*, meaning New Braunfels]. It is enough to make one explode when one has heard each and every one of the shop-keepers individually and sees their shameful souls lie fully exposed before one, and hears them sing 'War, Brother, War' in chorus."[37]

Yet with two sons still in the army, Coreth knew he had to demonstrate loyalty to the South. Although both Rudolf and Carl Coreth survived the Red River Campaign in the spring of 1864, their letters between April and July were infrequent. By the end of the year their correspondence reveals that neither brother felt the allegiance to the Confederacy that had encouraged them to enlist. Rudolf especially began to feel the rub of antiforeign sentiment. When the company elected a new lieutenant in December, Rudolf threw his name in as a candidate. There was no opposition until, as he told his father, "Lt. Bitter and his clique put up an American who has been in our company several weeks and made him my opponent. They kept after the men, and at the casting of votes he beat me by one vote. Almost all those who had asked me to run voted against me." One comrade told Coreth that he had not voted for him because he "thought it would make the company look very fine if we elected an American." As a result, Rudolf decided "to get out of the company and maybe even out of the army." His brother Carl felt the same way. Unfortunately for the Coreth family, Carl became sick and died in January, and a second brother was buried in an unmarked grave.[38]

The remaining Coreth son stayed in the army until the end of the war, but not without regrets. "It is horrifying that such great sacrifices have been made in the firm belief that something would be attained," Rudolf decided in May 1865, "and that it is now clear everything was in vain." Moreover, the family never recovered from its decision to support the Confederacy. That bitterness led several relatives to return to the land of their birth. Carl's wife and the baby son he never saw returned to Germany. Rudolf Coreth returned to Europe, where he died in 1901 in Vienna.[39]

Clearly German Texans had difficult decisions to make when the war came. They could join the Confederate army as the three Coreth brothers did, but their loyalty to a cause they did not fully support often waned as the sacrifice became too high to retain their allegiance. This was particularly true among Germans born in the Old World. Young men who had either been born in the United States or came as children often understood Texas culture better, for the state was a replica of its Southern neighbors, and those growing up in Texas often felt a strong loyalty to the Confederacy. Therefore, many German Texans fought loyally for the Confederacy. Those who opposed the Confederacy suffered the fate of dissenters throughout history; they either left or remained silent. Although all Confederate states had to deal with Unionists, most of the dissension came from Unionist Southerners themselves. Texas was the only Confederate state with a fairly large immigrant population that was seen as disloyal and the only state to pass laws aimed directly at that immigrant population.

Because of the divisions within the German communities, however, American-born Texans did not regard the various settlers with general antipathy. A large number of German-speaking Texans had fought loyally for the Confederacy and suffered along with other ex-Confederates during the Reconstruction years. Even though some immigrants chose to return to their homeland, many remained and others arrived. Between 1865 and the early 1890s, more German-speaking people immigrated to Texas than in the three decades prior to the war—perhaps as many as forty thousand. These new arrivals, however, generally avoided the Hill Country, the region where disaffection had centered in the war years. Texas even attracted Germans who had previously moved to the midwestern states, and as late as 1880, the population of San Antonio remained one-third German. As the world changed after 1900, so did German immigration to the

United States, and few came as Europe headed for its first world war. But the ones who had arrived in the nineteenth century played an important role in the cultural diversity and the rich cultural heritage of the Lone Star State.[40]

CHAPTER TWO

The War Within

The Divided Loyalties of Native Americans

The Civil War changed the lives of many Southerners forever. Before the war, for example, black Southerners had been largely left out of the political process, but after 1865 the U.S. government reassessed their legal status, and Americans of African descent became citizens; black males also gained the right to vote. Only one group of native-born Southerners remained entirely excluded from these basic rights and would remain excluded in some cases until the twentieth century. These people were the Natives whose ancestors had lived on the American continent for centuries. The war and the postwar years brought hardship and turmoil to the white residents of the eleven states that composed the Confederacy, as well as freedom for blacks, but for Native Americans little changed. The war proved to be just another chapter in their unequal relationship with the government of the United States, and later with that of the Confederacy, and a further example of broken promises, bad decisions, and unavoidable adversity.

For Native Americans living in the South in the decades before the war, much had already changed. The Indian Removal Act of 1830, passed by Congress and signed by President Andrew Jackson, had taken their ancestral homelands. Many Native Americans who lived east of the Mississippi River lost their land and liberties and were sent to the Indian Territory, an area that is now much of the state of Oklahoma. The federal government acquired millions of acres of fertile Southern soil, which it sold to speculators and settlers, thus allowing Euro-Americans to spread across the South. Although removal was harsh on the Southern tribes, they did not shed their Southern ties on arrival west of the Mississippi.

Five civilized tribes—the Cherokees, Chickasaws, Choctaws, Creeks, and Seminoles—made up the bulk of those removed to the Indian Territory under presidents Jackson and Martin Van Buren in the years following the removal act. The members of these tribes living on the eastern edge of the Indian Territory at the outbreak of the Civil War obviously interested presidents Abraham Lincoln and Jefferson Davis, and both wanted to obtain the tribes' loyalty. Personally, neither Lincoln nor Davis had much sympathy for the Indians. Lincoln believed in "white progress," and that did not include Native peoples. Davis had earlier pushed for the removal of Chickasaws and Choctaws from his home state of Mississippi.[1]

Before the war ended, some twenty thousand Native Americans served in the Confederate or Union armies. The Cherokee nation, with almost twenty-two thousand members, was the single most important tribe; some three thousand served in the Confederate army, and between eight thousand and thirteen thousand sympathized with the South. The Indian Territory provided Cherokees, Choctaws, Chickasaws, and Seminoles to the Confederacy and a brigade of Creeks to the Union. There were also Native Americans who served in regiments east of the Mississippi. A regiment from east Tennessee and western North Carolina, for example, had two companies composed largely of Cherokees. Names on the muster rolls of Rebel soldiers include such unexpected ones as Crying Bear, Spring Water, and Flying Bird.[2]

Some other Native Americans played a minor role in the Civil War. The Confederacy concluded treaties with several hostile Plains tribes, although both sides eventually broke those pacts. In Texas, for example, Kiowas and Comanches took advantage of the fact that the U.S. Army removed its cavalry from the forts along the western frontier, a line running roughly from San Antonio directly north to the Red River, the border with modern Oklahoma. Kiowas and Comanches raided as far east as the outskirts of Fort Worth, a growing settlement on the Trinity River. The state of Texas used frontier regiments to replace the U.S. cavalry in order to protect families living on the edge of settlement, but the Texas Rangers were not always successful at preventing attacks. Hostile Indians captured horses, cattle, and even, on occasion, women and children. This, of course, had the expected result, as soldiers in the Confederate army often took "french leave," or temporarily went AWOL, to learn what was happening at home. In the spring of 1863, for instance, a company of Texas cavalry stationed in southern Arkansas left camp and headed west after hearing of Indian raids along the Texas frontier. When the company's lieutenant was asked to stop the men, he replied that it would be useless to try; he knew the men and knew they would continue homeward until they learned the truth about the Indian attacks. Still, the lieutenant remained convinced that the soldiers would return to duty as soon as they determined their families were safe. Unofficially and without permission, several hundred men left for home. Once they discovered that the stories of the Indian atrocities were nothing but exaggerated rumors, they returned to the army. Apparently the authorities ordered no punishment for any of them.[3]

Texas had a peculiar relationship with various Indian tribes. It was the only Confederate state with an active Indian frontier, and when Texans wrote their ordinance of secession, the Indian issue was one of the reasons given as justification for leaving the Union. Long before Texas became a state, authorities, whether Spanish, Mexican, or American, had had to deal with the tribes that called the American Southwest their home. Unfriendly Plains tribes, such as Comanches, Apaches, and Kiowas, inhabited the western reaches of Texas. Cherokees, Choctaws, Alabamas, and Coushattas, at the encouragement of Spain, had settled in east Texas in the early nineteenth century. When U.S. settlers began arriving from the Southern states, Texas Cherokees in particular had sought to live with them peaceably, but in spite of loyalty to Mexico, and later to the Americans, they were driven from Texas in 1839.

It was Georgia-born Mirabeau B. Lamar who repudiated the treaty of 1836 between the Cherokee tribe and the Republic of Texas, resulting in a war and expulsion of that tribe to land north of the Red River. Lamar was a Southerner who believed Native Americans did not fit into a prosperous plantation-based culture. Born near Louisville, Georgia, he had grown up on his father's plantation near Milledgeville. He attended academies at Milledgeville and Eatonton and as a young adult married a woman from Twiggs County. He became a newspaper editor in Columbus and, after failing in politics in Georgia, followed a friend to Texas. Elected vice president of the new republic in 1836, he spent much of the following year back in Georgia being treated as a hero at parties thrown by high society's elite. In 1838, he was elected president of the Republic and began a program to create a Texas in the image of his home state complete with institutions of higher learning, a modern economy, and gracious plantations. Native Americans blemished this vision, so Lamar wanted to apply the Georgia model of expulsion to Texas Cherokees. Instead of Sam Houston's conciliatory policy toward the Indians, Lamar fashioned one of annihilation and displacement that eventually resulted in the Cherokee removal. This corresponded nicely with the U.S. government's policy aimed at removing the five civilized tribes from the American Southeast.[4]

Ultimately only the Alabama and Coushatta tribes remained at peace in Texas, under a treaty ratified in 1840. The Alabama-Coushatta had the ability to deal diplomatically with the state of Texas and by 1854 had received a permanent home in Polk County, northeast of Houston. Many of the young men from the Alabama and Coushatta tribes as well as one or two Muscogees joined the Confederate army. One company had sixty-four Indians and sixty-nine white men, mostly reformed deserters. The muster rolls indicate that most of these Indians adopted Americanized names that would not distinguish them from their comrades of European ancestry. On the muster they signed as Bill, Bob, Charley, Jack, Jim, Joe, or John. There was no last name, and nothing indicated who they were except the designation Alabama Indian or Coushatta Indian. Others carried Americanized names such as Dick Connor and John Thompson; both of these men were from the Alabama tribe. There was no thought of actually sending them into battle in a white man's war; instead the captain suggested using the Alabama-Coushatta Indians as scouts in the swamps and canebrakes of southern Louisiana because a branch of the tribes lived near Opelousas. Most Southern states placed Indians in the same category as free blacks. North Carolina, for example, passed a law in 1835 redefining Indians as "free persons of color." The fact that the Confederacy would only group the Indians with whites who had been arrested for desertion is a telling analysis of government policy.[5]

At the outbreak of the war, the Confederacy's Indian problem was twofold. While Confederate ambassadors wanted to encourage as many tribes as possible to join in the Southern war for independence, the new government also had to protect Confederates on the western frontier from attacks from hostile Plains tribes. The Union had similar problems. The U.S. government wanted to persuade Indian leaders to support the Union, but unfriendly Sioux and Navajos led to concerns for settlers in the American West. The Navajos, for example, had caused trouble since the war with Mexico began in 1846 when U.S. soldiers moved into the region that later became the states of New Mexico and Arizona. In fact, Colonel "Kit" Carson became a hero for using a "scorched earth" policy to round up and subdue some eight thousand Navajos in late 1863 and early 1864.[6]

At the same time, Sioux uprisings in Minnesota increased in frequency and intensity. General John Pope, who commanded the Union army in the Second Battle of Bull Run, was placed in charge of the Department of the Northwest in late 1862 to deal with the problem. Although feeling he had been banished to Minnesota by President Lincoln for his failure to defeat the Confederate army under Robert E. Lee, in his exile he became known as the army's Indian expert, particularly for his previous dealings with Indians in New Mexico in the 1850s and in the Northwest during the Civil War. His support for reservations, where the hostile Indians could be exposed to "Christianity and education," would do little to quell the insurgency, however. During the summer of 1862 warfare swept across the Minnesota-Dakota borderlands, where starving Santee Sioux rebelled against the policies of the traders and protested corrupt policies. Following a bloody uprising more than three hundred Indians and half-breeds were scheduled for execution. Lincoln reviewed the verdicts, and eventually only thirty-eight Indians, those found guilty of rape or murder, were hanged. Three, it turned out, were hanged by mistake. Others went to prison, and the army moved the remainder of the tribe further west.[7]

Still, Union and Confederate representatives continued to establish treaties with both hostile and friendly tribes, although only the Confederacy took positive steps to secure the loyalty of the Indian Territory's estimated one hundred thousand inhabitants. For the Confederacy the most significant gains came with the five civilized tribes in the Indian Territory. To the north of the Indian Territory was the free state of Kansas, the battleground over slavery in the decade of the 1850s. To the east lay Confederate Arkansas and to the northeast, Missouri, a slave state that remained loyal to the Union. To the south was the Lone Star State. This strategic location meant that neutrality would be hard. Because the Indian Territory sat directly between Confederate Texas and Unionist Kansas, it was of particular importance to Texans, for they needed a military buffer to protect the northern settlements: That geographical screen was land belonging to the Creeks, Choctaws, Chickasaws, Seminoles, and Cherokees, tribes that had settled in the eastern Indian Territory in the 1830s. As soon as the eventuality of war became obvious, the Confederate government appointed commissioners to travel to the Indian Territory to speak, in particular, to the Cherokees. From Arkansas, the governor, Henry M. Rector, and his cousin, Elias Rector, superintendent of Indian Affairs at Fort Smith, went directly to John Ross, chief of the Cherokee nation.[8]

To understand the Native Americans in the Indian Territory in 1861, one must turn back the clock several decades and consider what had occurred when white settlers encroached on tribal lands across the South. Born in 1790 and only one-eighth Cherokee, John Ross had lived in northern Georgia before the banishment of his tribe. He had fought in the Creek War and had met such notables as Sam Houston. He had also been one of the richest men in north Georgia, with a two-hundred-acre farm and many slaves. After he became a leader of his tribe, he frequently visited the national capital of Washington and negotiated treaties with the federal government, and he was among the Cherokee leaders who tried to use the legal system to prevent the forced removal of the tribe. In an attempt to become more Americanized, the Cherokees organized as a nation and wrote a constitution based on that of the United States. Ross served as president of the constitutional convention and won election as principal chief, a position he held—with the exception of the split during the Civil War—until he died in 1866. But Ross's opposition, a group known as the Treaty Party, signed away the Cherokee lands in Georgia in 1835 for five million dollars, seven million acres west of the Mississippi River, and a promise to move within two years. Although Ross obtained signatures in opposition to the treaty from sixteen thousand of the approximately seventeen thousand Cherokees who lived in Georgia, President Jackson ignored their pleas.[9]

The institution of slavery accompanied the Cherokees, Chickasaws, and Choctaws to the Indian Territory. These tribes included wealthy slaveholders who identified with the white culture as they distanced themselves from the African American race. Some four thousand slaves lived in the Indian Territory at the time of the Civil War, even though only an estimated 2.3 percent of Native Americans owned slaves. Yet, like political leaders in the Southern states, slaveholders dominated the tribal governments, and laws regarding slaves in the Indian Territory were similar to those in the South.[10]

Still, there was no consensus among Native Americans over slavery. Many traditional Indians saw it as incompatible with their ancestral heritage. Florida Seminoles had even allowed escaped slaves to live among them, and that relationship continued after removal to the West. Black Seminoles feared the tribes that held slaves, and the Creeks and Cherokees did not want to live alongside free black Seminoles. The problem was solved in 1855 with the creation of a separate Seminole nation within the Indian Territory.[11]

Divisions within the tribes of the Indian nation could be traced back to Jackson's removal policy and in particular to the Cherokees in Georgia. For most Americans the best-known Indian during the Civil War was Georgia-born Confederate general Stand Watie. The Georgian's commanding officer once noted of the only Native American to rise to the rank of brigadier general, "I wish I had as much energy in some of my white commanders as he displays."[12]

Watie's father was a full-blooded Cherokee and his mother a half blood. Born near Rome, Georgia, in December 1806, Stand Watie was fifty-four years old when the war broke out. As a product of two cultures, he had received an education at a Moravian mission school and eventually joined the Moravian Church. He finished his education at the Foreign Mission School in Cornwall, Connecticut, before returning to north Georgia to become a planter. Watie served as a clerk of the Cherokee Supreme Court and as the speaker of the Cherokee National Council, and his brother Buck Watie was named editor of the *Cherokee Phoenix*, the tribal newspaper. In fact, Buck Watie is an example of how acculturated the Cherokee had become by the time of the war. When he went to school in Connecticut, he took the name of his Philadelphia benefactor, Elias Boudinot. He even married a Connecticut woman.[13]

As a member of the Ridge-Watie-Boudinot faction of the Cherokee nation, Stand Watie was one of the men to sign the Treaty of New Echota in 1835, and he moved to the Indian Territory shortly thereafter, settling at Honey Creek. Like other signers of the treaty that forfeited tribal lands, Watie put himself in danger by placing his name on the unpopular document. The "Trail of Tears" did nothing to improve relations within the Cherokee nation, and within six months of removal conservative Cherokees executed three of the signers of the Treaty of New Echota: Watie's uncle, seventy-year-old Major Ridge, cousin John Ridge, and brother Elias Boudinot (Buck Watie). Major Ridge was shot while on his way to Arkansas; his son John was murdered in front of his Connecticut-born wife and their children; and Elias Boudinot was executed shortly after leaving a friend's house. In 1845 Stand Watie's brother Thomas and friend James Starr were murdered. These assassinations led to an intratribal war similar to a blood feud that lasted until a treaty the following year brought about an uneasy truce. Watie, who survived the assassination plot in 1839 and several subsequent attempts to murder him, became leader of the Ridge-Watie-Boudinot faction of the tribe in direct opposition to John Ross's full-blooded faction. Yet the Ross faction outnumbered the Ridge party and still held political power at the time of the Civil War.[14]

Watie was a Southerner in a surrounding that could hardly be called typically Southern. The extreme northeastern Indian Territory was mountainous and seemed an unlikely spot for a plantation-based society. It was, however, very similar to the mountains of north Georgia he had left as a young man. Moreover, the hills soon gave way to level plains that could be farmed. Watie became a Southern slaveholder and lived like a white middle-class Southerner. He even organized a branch of the Knights of the Golden Circle, a radical organization dedicated to Southern rights and opposed to abolition. Not surprisingly, he allied with the Confederacy when the war began, and he raised a company of like-minded Cherokees in spite of Ross's efforts to keep the tribe neutral.

Because the Cherokee nation was the most powerful in the Indian Territory, convincing the Cherokees to join the Confederacy would mean that other tribes would probably follow. But Ross felt that the quarrels between the North and South meant nothing to the Indians, and he displayed little interest in a Cherokee-Confederate alliance. Ross was seventy-one years old at the time the secession crisis broke the nation apart, and he was too experienced to be swayed by empty promises from either side. Ross understood that, on one hand, the Indians relied on the federal government for sustenance and many tribal members had suffered greatly from a recent drought that had devastated crops. Moreover, the tribes had not received all the money promised by the U.S. government following removal from the Southeast. On the other hand, rumors abounded that one of the presidential hopefuls in 1860, William H. Seward, showed little concern for the plight of the Indians and had even observed that the territory "south of Kansas must be vacated by the Indian." Moreover, once the war began, peaceful Indians, like the white settlers in west Texas, suffered when the U.S. Army evacuated the posts on the western frontier. Like the white Texans, the Cherokees and other peaceful tribes were left defenseless against the hostile Plains tribes. In addition, the U.S. Army evacuated Fort Smith, Arkansas, which served as a federal supply depot, and Confederate forces soon moved into the town. After Texas general Ben McCulloch arrived, he planned to move Confederate forces into the Cherokee nation to create a buffer between Texas and Kansas. Nonetheless, Ross objected and issued a proclamation of neutrality on May 17, 1861.[15]

More than a concern for his tribe affected Ross's position. Ross's second wife, Mary, was Northern born. She was a Delaware Quaker whom he had married when he was fifty-four and she just eighteen. Not only did Northern missionaries want the Cherokees to remain neutral, Ross apparently hesitated to alienate his wife's family in the North. In fact, the entire situation was as complicated as any divisions that occur during civil wars. There were Cherokees who disliked white Southerners, particularly those who had taken their lands in Georgia, Alabama, and elsewhere. There were Cherokees who disliked Texans because of the trouble under the Republic of Texas. There were Cherokees who disliked each other, divided between those who opposed slavery and those who held slaves. But underlying everything was the hatred that still simmered over the Treaty of New Echota of 1835. Cherokees had long memories and, perhaps even more significant in this case, long life spans.[16]

Into this political quagmire stepped Massachusetts-born Albert Pike, who was appointed the Confederate special commissioner to the Indian tribes. Pike had adopted Arkansas as his home and, as a lawyer, had represented various Indians in legal cases in the 1850s that went as far as the U.S. Supreme Court. In 1839, during the removal, John Ross's first wife Elizabeth had died at Little Rock and was buried in a cemetery plot belonging to Pike. Because the two men had been friends for many years, Pike was able to meet with Ross in May 1861 and persuade the chief to call a meeting of the tribe to discuss the situation.[17]

The Cherokees met at their capital of Tahlequah on August 21 to discuss their thoughts and positions on the current crisis. Around four thousand attended, mostly men, "whose deportment," it was said, "was characterized by good order and propriety, and the expression of whose opinions and feelings was frank, cordial, and of marked unanimity." Chief Ross told the crowd that their "precious rights" were at stake and that their "posterity" would be affected by the decisions they would make. He noted that "evil times ha[d] befallen the great Government with which [they had] been connected" but pointed out that the relationship with the United States, sealed by treaty in the 1830s, still existed. He pleaded for the Cherokees to avoid conflict with either the United States or the Confederate States but admitted that it would be difficult. In the final vote, resolutions in support of the Confederate States carried by acclamation.[18]

Chief Ross submitted to the will of his people, and events moved rapidly following the decision. On October 7 tribal leaders signed an official treaty with the Confederate government, and the Confederate Congress ratified the document in December. Ross was never enthusiastic about this decision, but he did feel as if the Union had abandoned his people. Possibly, and certainly central to his person, Ross had lost any military protection that the U.S. Army had provided him from Watie and his followers. He also knew that his supporters were unhappy that the federal government had declined to pay annuities because it claimed that most tribes in the Indian Territory had already joined the Confederacy. In fact, during this critical period, the federal government unintentionally helped the South by abandoning several forts, leaving the eastern Indian Territory open to white intruders and the western region unprotected from hostile Plains Indians. Both withdrawing soldiers and withholding annuities violated the removal treaties of the 1830s.[19]

In return for a treaty of alliance, the Confederacy promised that the Cherokees would never lose their lands and pledged to provide adequate arms and ammunition needed for protection of those lands. Indians would also receive the same pay as regular Confederate soldiers. Although a provision in the treaty guaranteed that Cherokees would not be asked to fight beyond their borders, the Confederacy violated this promise several times during the war. As soon as the alliance became official, Pike took command of the military district of the Indian Territory and established Fort Davis at the old Union Fort Gibson.

At the same time, the Confederacy had to deal with divisions within the Creek nation. Historians still debate the causes of the factionalism. Some make geographical distinctions dating back to the tribe's days in Alabama stating that the pro-Confederate Creeks were the old Lower Creek composed of the more acculturated mixed bloods while the ones who supported the Union came from the traditionalist full-bloods of the Upper Creek faction. Some recent ethnohistorians have blamed the divisions on the introduction of slavery; others say that simple tradition within Creek factions is a possible explanation. In spite of the amount of discussion, no one has adequately explained the cause.[20]

Divisions within the various tribes, along with the success of the Confederate government at concluding treaties with sympathetic tribal leaders, encouraged Unionists Indians to leave the Indian Territory. In late 1862 some seven thousand to eight thousand refugees from the Creek and Seminole tribes, including women and children, with a few black followers, headed for Kansas. Confederate Creeks attacked the fleeing columns, and although Union Indians won the first two engagements, the Confederates prevailed in what became known as the Battle of Chustenahlah. The Indians' civil war, a war within a war, had begun in earnest. Following the Battle of Chustenahlah those Indians who made it safely to Kansas soon donned the Union blue and returned to fight in their homeland for the United States. When this happened, the conflict in the Indian Territory deteriorated into bloody guerrilla warfare.[21]

At the outset of the war, events in the Indian Territory meant nothing to the average Southerner. Regardless of how "civilized" the Cherokees or Creeks were, to most Southerners they would always be "Indians," and Indians, as most Americans thought, were hostile and dangerous. By 1861 the stereotype of the "red man" with bow and arrow had already become part of American folklore. Indians, like slaves, were not citizens, but if one examined the portrait of a man like Ross, one would see a typical Southern gentleman. His home, Rose Cottage, in the Indian Territory, was a two-story mansion with four huge white columns. Around ten thousand dollars of furniture had been shipped from the East, and the plantation, worked by slaves, spanned a thousand acres and "was immensely profitable."[22]

But when the fighting started, all eyes followed the battles in Virginia, where the North and South first clashed at Manassas Junction on Bull Run Creek in the summer of 1861, not the battles in the West. Few noticed when Stand Watie's battalion fought in the Battle of Wilson's Creek in August 1861. This battle, in southwestern Missouri, was a tactical Southern victory but a strategic loss, as the Confederates vacated Missouri for northwest Arkansas. The Indians' main contribution in the battle seems to have been a frightening war whoop that when added to the Rebel yell had the intended paralyzing effect on the enemy.[23]

At about this same time, John Drew, a Ross man, raised a regiment primarily of full-bloods and former Unionist Indians. Colonel Drew was in his midsixties, so his campaigning was somewhat limited. The lieutenant colonel, William Potter Ross, was both a graduate of Princeton College and the nephew of Chief Ross. In fact, many of the officers were educated half-breeds and direct relatives of Ross. Drew himself was married to Ross's niece. Although the Confederate Cherokees may have seemed united on the Southern side, there was fear that the men under Stand Watie and those under Drew would clash. Both called their command the First Regiment of Cherokee Mounted Rifles, and the only way to avoid confusion was to refer to each force by the name of the commander. In fact, Watie expanded his battalion into a regiment in part to match Drew's regiment. The animosity, born in Georgia, now divided the Cherokees into two armed camps, united only on paper against the common Northern invader.[24]

In fact, these old divisions had reemerged just before the outbreak of war. Within the Cherokee tribe was the Keetoowah Society, a secret organization that had as one of its goals the preservation of traditional tribal values. Members were uneducated full-blooded Cherokees who had no mixed-blood friends, and the fraternal organization used the punishment of death for revealing secrets. Many members of the society even joined a secret Loyal League, organized in late 1860 or 1861. The goal of both seems to have been the abolition of slavery and the continued dominance of the Ross party over tribal politics. Because they wore distinctive pins on their coat lapels or shirts, they earned the name Pin Indians, but before the war ended, the name Pin came to refer to Union Indians in general. Many of the enlisted men in Drew's regiment came from this base.[25]

In opposition were the men in Stand Watie's regiment. Georgia-born Watie did not try to be a Southern cavalier. He wore simple clothing: a black slouch hat, a plain plantation coat, gray flannel trousers, and knee-high riding boots. He looked neither like an Indian nor like a Confederate soldier. A contemporary photograph shows a man with short white hair who only slightly resembled the image most Americans had of an Indian. His third wife, Sarah, born in the old Cherokee nation east of the Mississippi, as well as the couple's children, looked even less like the stereotype that contemporaries had of Native Americans; intermarriage with whites during the years in Georgia had Americanized many Cherokee. Yet Watie was as good a Cherokee Confederate as would be seen in the Indian Territory, and he weathered many controversies that befell the Confederate tribes.[26]

The single most publicized event involving these Native Americans came in March 1862 at the Battle of Pea Ridge, Arkansas. The fighting, lasting from the sixth through the eighth, proved more like mob violence than a battle between trained armies. Moreover, following the fighting, accusations surfaced of the scalping of dead and wounded Union soldiers. Union victor General Samuel R. Curtis wrote the Confederate commander Earl Van Dorn, "The general regrets that we find on the battle-field, contrary to civilized warfare, many of the Federal dead who were tomahawked, scalped, and their bodies shamefully mangled, and expresses a hope that this important struggle may not degenerate to a savage warfare." Curtis repeated this charge several times, singling out Albert Pike's soldiers. "General Pike," he noted, "commanded the Indian forces. They shot arrows as well as rifles, and tomahawked and scalped prisoners."[27]

Historians Bill Shea and Earl Hess believe that the worst legacy "in the minds of Civil War contemporaries—and the most exotic in the minds of present-day students"—was how posterity remembered their actions. Pea Ridge was the only significant battle that involved Indians, and accounts of the atrocities both fascinated and shocked Northerners. An Illinois soldier told his wife: "These Indians are blood thirsty and savage. We know when we fight them that we have to fight on a different principle than we would white men. We must be constantly on our guard as if we were fighting wildcats." Another noted, "There will be no quarter shown them after this, that is certain."[28]

Confederate commander Earl Van Dorn said he was "pained" to hear reports of soldiers who had been "scalped, tomahawked, and otherwise mutilated." Van Dorn reminded the Union general that the Indians in his army had "for many years been regarded as civilized people." In an attempt to steer the charges of these outrages away from the Native Americans, Van Dorn pointed out that he had heard of Confederate prisoners who were "murdered in cold blood by their captors." The villains in this case were German soldiers, and Van Dorn wrote the Union commander that he hoped that they would both do their part in "preventing such atrocities in [the] future, and that the perpetrators" of such atrocities would "be brought to justice, whether German or Choctaw." Clearly, racial bigotry was not confined to Native peoples, as Van Dorn included Hessians, or German-Unionist soldiers whom Confederates labeled as "Dutch," in his countercondemnation. A large number of Germans, whom the Union had recruited in Saint Louis, served in the western armies fighting in Missouri and Arkansas.[29]

The controversy over Pea Ridge and Indian troop use reached all the way to the halls of Congress in Washington, D.C. An investigation by the Joint Congressional Committee on the Conduct of the War proved strongly critical of the use of Indians in battle. Words like "savages," "barbarity," and "merciless" surfaced during the discussions when describing the scalpings and mutilations. Even Confederates strongly condemned such actions. The result was Pike's resignation, as he could not disassociate himself from the murders at Pea Ridge. In fact, for decades following the war, partisans from the Indian regiments involved in the battle blamed each other for the atrocities, and the debate continues to this day.[30]

Without doubt, the Civil War provided restless young Indian males an opportunity that had long been lost to those tribes that had adopted white ways. Members of the five civilized tribes had for the most part absorbed white lifestyles; many of the young men went to school in the North and had learned how to survive in a white world. The changing times of the mid-1800s no longer offered traditional ways of marking manhood. Gone were the days of becoming a warrior through military prowess in battle. Except for an occasional fight with hostile Plains Indians, these restless young men had few outlets for their energy. The established means of achieving status as a leader of men in battle were rare, so the coming of the Civil War provided opportunities that had not existed for decades. Not surprisingly, young Indian men both dressed the part of warrior and occasionally acted out the role that white society expected from them.

The elder generation could remember a time when preparing for war was common, and the younger generation was anxious to follow in these tribal traditions. But not everyone was happy with the situation. Soon after Chief Ross allied the Cherokees with the Confederacy, he decided he had made a mistake; unfortunately he could see no way of changing his allegiance without staining his honor. The U.S. Army provided Ross an acceptable way out of his dilemma. After a Union patrol entered his yard and captured him in his comfortable home at Tahlequah, he left the Indian Territory as a prisoner of war. He packed up his family and the Cherokee treasury and archives and headed for Kansas. The old chief died in Washington, D.C., four years later. (Incidentally, just ten days after Ross died, the U.S. Senate ratified a new postwar treaty with the Cherokees.) After Ross's defection in 1862 Watie became principal chief of the Confederate Cherokees. The Cherokees' internal war did not end just because Ross had fled, however; in fact it intensified. Watie led vindictive raids against Ross's remaining supporters as well as federal soldiers, and in one raid Ross's fine home was burned to the ground.[31]

A report sent to the Confederate secretary of war in 1862 noted the widening guerrilla war. The commissioner observed that a "spirit of dissatisfaction" pervaded the various tribes because of the failure of the Confederate government to hold to its part of the treaties. The document stated that only the Choctaws had remained perfectly united in their loyalty to the Confederate government while the Chickasaws had lost about forty families. Around one-half of the Seminoles had allied with the North, although their chief, John Jumper, had displayed "unshaken fidelity to the Confederate cause." The report estimated that the Creeks had lost about a thousand or fifteen hundred of their people but noted that Stand Watie had a large following in the Cherokee nation. Although numerous other tribes were canvassed, the five civilized tribes were the ones that both the Union and Confederate governments generally referred to when dealing with Native Americans.[32]

Still, historians tend to overlook one vital point when studying the Civil War in the Indian Territory. Too often it is easy to separate the quarrels within the various Indian nations from the war itself. And it is easy to forget that many of the Southern troops serving in the Indian Territory were white Confederates from Texas. These Confederates arrived north of the Red River with strong prejudices based on experiences with hostile tribes on the Texas frontier and unimpressed with advances among the Cherokees and Creeks. As the war progressed, these prejudices grew, particularly among soldiers from the western frontier of Texas, and strained relations between some of the white Confederate soldiers and Native American Confederates.

Most Texans knew the story of Cynthia Ann Parker, for newspapers had carried the tale just as tabloids would today. A raiding party of Comanches had captured Parker as a child, along with four others. Although the others were eventually released, Cynthia Ann was held for twenty-five years. She married, had children, and refused to return to white society when traders tried to persuade her to leave the tribe. But in December 1860, Texas Rangers attacked a small Comanche hunting party and took three captives; among them they found a blue-eyed woman and a small child. The woman was Cynthia Ann Parker. Much to the surprise of her white relatives, she spurned white society and tried, on several occasions, to escape back to her husband and grown sons. On April 8, 1861, just days before the firing on Fort Sumter started the Civil War, the Texas legislature voted her a pension of one hundred dollars annually for five years and a generous land grant, a gift she neither asked for nor wanted. She died without seeing her Comanche family again. But Texans associated Native peoples in the Indian Territory only with the terrifying elements of such stories: There was no sympathy for Native Americans who scalped, murdered, raped, or kidnapped white children.[33]

Such atrocities continued during the war. In the spring of 1861 hostile Indians murdered several white settlers in Parker County, to the northwest of Fort Worth. Later in the summer a woman was scalped, "killed on the spot," by what were described as "savage monsters." Stories like these grew in the retelling, and separating myth from fact became impossible.[34]

Although the Indians generally only wanted to steal horses and cattle, in some instances they did capture or murder women and children. Families along the Confederacy's western frontier moved in together, and lines between friendly and hostile Indians blurred. At Thorp Spring, west of Fort Worth, families lived in tents along the creek, and it was possible to see "fifty or a hundred tents" housing women and children with no male head of house present. The Texas soldiers stationed in the Indian Territory felt little sympathy for the Indian Confederates, and relations suffered as a result.[35]

No one had any intention of placing white soldiers under an Indian commander, but white Texans did have to live among Native Americans when northeast Texas became home to thousands of refugees from the Indian Territory. After the Cherokee nation fell into Union hands, Cherokees with Southern sympathies moved south, including Watie's own family. The Indian Territory became a battleground filled not only with soldiers from both sides but also with jayhawkers, guerrillas, and just plain outlaws. Colonel Douglas Hancock Cooper, from the Indian Territory, authorized the use of the Choctaw and Chickasaw Mounted Rifles against hostile Indians and jayhawkers. Added to this violence were the partisan murders resulting from removal era hostilities. Civilians, whether they supported the North or the South, fled to Confederate outposts or across the Red River into Texas. Wealthy pro-Confederate Indian families took livestock and valuable slaves out of harm's way.

With each passing year the violence escalated and more civilians became displaced. In the summer of 1862 a Union invasion from Kansas, known as the Indian Expedition, sent pro-Confederate Cherokees fleeing into the Creek nation before the federal columns withdrew. In April 1863 another invasion from Kansas included soldiers who had been slaves as well as Indians wearing Union blue. These soldiers burned homes in a personal vendetta that had little do to with the war between Rebels and Yankees. After the Battle of Honey Springs in July 1863, pro-Confederate Creek and Cherokee civilians fled in an exodus later dubbed "the Stampede." The Cherokee nation became a Union stronghold, and few people inhabited the Creek nation in the last two years of the war.

Feeding the refugees fell to the Confederate government. At one point, there were an estimated 2,906 Cherokees at Tishomingo, 574 Seminoles near Fort Washita, 241 Osages near Fort Arbuckle, and 4,480 Choctaws and 785 Chickasaws in other scattered locations, as well as several other Indian groups and camps, for a total of 13,809. Because providing for Confederate soldiers and mounts strained the resources of Trans-Mississippi Confederates, Indian civilian refugees predictably did not fare well.[36]

One might assume that Indian refugees to Union-held posts would enjoy better conditions. Certainly the federal government had the resources and the experience; the U.S. government ran contraband camps, or camps for freed slaves, all across the occupied South. The number of free black men and women living in these facilities could exceed thousands. But Northern abolitionists kept a close eye on the contraband camps, for this was the experiment in freedom that they had long advocated. New England societies sent teachers and worked to teach freed slaves to read and write. By contrast, most missionaries had fled the Indian Territory early in the war, and few were left to lobby for the refugees. In 1862 some 5,487 Native American refugees suffered in squalid surroundings in Kansas. Although some pro-Union Indians returned to the Indian Territory with the Union army after Fort Gibson fell, they rarely left the protection offered by Northern cannon. Following the Confederate loss at Honey Springs, freed slaves raised the number of people needing government assistance, and malnutrition and disease spread, making life miserable.[37]

By late 1863 even Stand Watie had become discouraged. After enemy forces occupied the Cherokee nation, he wrote the following to the governors of the Choctaw and Chickasaw nations: "Relief and protection, so often cheeringly promised [from the Confederate government], have never been afforded us, and, from present indications, I see no prospects of efficient aid outside of the Indian country. Every day seems to drive conviction to my heart that we, the Indians still true to the South, must place small reliance on assistance . . . , but must test our whole power to defend our homes and firesides." He felt not only that Richmond authorities had cast aside the Indian Territory but also that Confederate commanders in the Trans-Mississippi Department showed little interest in helping the Cherokees regain their homes, and he added, "I am loath to believe that the Confederate authorities have entirely abandoned the Cherokee country, but I see in the future scarcely a ray of hope from them." Finally, he issued a warning to the other tribes, concluding, "If the Cherokee nation is abandoned to the enemy, the Creek country falls the next victim, and in speedy turn [all the other] Nations will share the same fate."[38]

Prejudices against Native Americans thrived in the far West also. In November 1864, at the same time General William T. Sherman was marching across Georgia and on the eve of the Battle of Franklin in Tennessee, Colonel John M. Chivington led one thousand men from the Third Colorado Volunteers in an attack on some five hundred sleeping Cheyennes. The Indians, believing that a peace treaty was in effect, had turned their arms in at Fort Lyon, Colorado. The soldiers slaughtered men, women, and children; around one hundred and fifty died, and some were mutilated. After the victory, the white soldiers brought scalps back to Denver, displaying them as trophies of war, and white civilians applauded their success. Although the U.S. Congress investigated what became known as the Sand Creek Massacre, no one was punished, for Chivington had left the army, and few white Americans cared what happened to the Indians as the nation's great national conflict drew to a close.[39]

Moreover, as with other minorities in the South during the Civil War, there was little interest after the fighting ended in the contribution of the Confederate Indians. Slaveholding Native Americans lost everything and had to sit by while their slaves, now free, received citizenship and the right to vote, a privilege not extended to all Native peoples until the early twentieth century. In addition, the emergence of the Lost Cause following the war meant that few people wanted to hear about the exploits of men who were not white native-born soldiers with roots in the British Isles. The Confederates of the 1870s and after became gallant cavaliers such as Robert E. Lee, Stonewall Jackson, and J. E. B. Stuart; even Ulysses S. Grant, William T. Sherman, and Philip Sheridan became larger than life. With the official closing of the frontier in 1890 and the containment of hostile Indian tribes on reservations, no one wanted to remember the exploits or accomplishments of Confederate Indians. If any stories surfaced at all, they were often related to tales of scalpings and other atrocities at the Battle of Pea Ridge.

Some fifty years following the war, Watie's grandniece, Mabel W. Anderson, wrote a short biography that included only one chapter on Watie's war years. Not until 1959 did a critical study of Native Americans emerge when Frank Cunningham published *General Stand Watie's Confederate Indians*. The book did not focus on Watie but looked at the contribution of the five civilized tribes to the Confederate cause. Although Cunningham's work displayed a decided Southern bias on the eve of the centennial of the Civil War, Cunningham was the first to detail the role of Confederate Indians. A mix of legends, myths, and folklore, the book provided a colorful story, but its publication also highlighted what little credible work had emerged on Confederate Indians by the time of the 1960s centennial celebrations. Fortunately that has changed some in recent years.[40]

The importance of the Indian Territory cannot be underestimated. Confederate Indians and Confederate Texans held firm above the Red River. They succeeded in the original objective, which was to provide a buffer for Texas through which Union armies could not pass. Without this buffer, enemy columns could have easily marched from Kansas into North Texas. For the first two years of the war, Texas provided beef cattle for Confederate armies east of the Mississippi River, and military supplies procured from Europe came in through Mexico. The loss of Texas would have had a significantly negative effect on the Confederate war effort. To provide such a buffer, Native Americans endured displacement, disease, and death. It is estimated that the dead and missing ranged from one of nine Chickasaws to one of every four Creeks. A census taken before and after the war indicated a decline in the Creek population of about 24 percent, the highest death rate among the five civilized tribes. Cherokees experienced great losses as well.[41]

The Indian Territory suffered great devastation from the war, particularly the settlements of the Cherokees and the Creeks. The Cherokee nation was left in shambles, while Creek public buildings and schools had been vandalized and looted. All the livestock was gone, eaten by refugees or taken by Union or Confederate soldiers. One Creek observed that all that remained was the land, "and that was because, of all Creek property, only the land was immovable."[42]

Moreover, when the war was over, it seemed not to matter which government the tribes had supported. Tribes that had been united in their support of the Confederacy often endured the least humiliating Reconstruction terms, and those that had supported the Union often suffered the most. Soon after the war ended, the U.S. government held its first conference with the various tribes. Federal officials informed the Native Americans that by supporting the Confederacy they had "forfeited all *rights*" gained from previous treaties and that they would be "at the mercy of the government." In general terms that meant that they had no choice but to accept Reconstruction treaties. The Choctaws and Chickasaws had to sell a region known as the Leased District to the United States for three hundred thousand dollars, and the Creeks had to cede all of the western part of their territory, more than three million acres, for fewer than one million dollars, or about thirty cents per acre. The Seminoles, the smallest of the five civilized tribes, had to sell all of their two million acres for fifteen cents per acre. They were allowed to buy over two hundred thousand acres of Creek land, but they had to pay fifty cents per acre for land the government had only paid the Creeks thirty cents an acre for. Moreover, the Cherokees had to sell more than six million acres, later known as the Cherokee strip, to the federal government and in return did not even receive the promised adjustments. The federal government considered the entire Cherokee nation disloyal.[43]

Following the war, white settlers moved into the Indian Territory in increasing numbers; many of these new inhabitants were Civil War veterans looking for a new start. In 1907 the remaining area became the state of Oklahoma, which is a Choctaw word meaning "Red Man" or "Red People." For the Native Americans the war was just another chapter in a long list of events that left the Native peoples again at the mercy of a white government that did not always have their best interest at heart. Certainly the U.S. government did not have a history of satisfactory dealings with Native peoples, but as it turned out, the Confederate government was unable to do much better. In the final analysis, Native Americans stood to lose no matter what they did. Even their contribution to the war was forgotten. A census in 1867 showed a Cherokee population of 13,566 as compared to twenty-one thousand in 1860; one-third of that nation had died during the four years of war. Outlaws, renegades, vigilantes, and soldiers from both sides had ravaged the countryside. But Native Americans, unable to leave the reservation, had nowhere else to go. They had to rebuild in the face of adversity, their battles with the federal government still unresolved.

CHAPTER THREE

In the Cause of Freedom

Southern Blacks in a Northern Army

When Southerners drafted the Constitution of the Confederate States of America, they chose to pattern it on the one that had worked for the United States for the previous seven decades. One obvious difference, however, was that the Confederate constitution protected the institution of slavery. Slaves remained property, and state laws regarding slavery did not change; it was still unlawful for a slave to carry a weapon. As a result of this decision the Confederacy rejected the possibility of using black males in military combat roles. Yet the new Confederate president received letters from blacks, both slave and free, requesting to join the army. In early April one Georgia regiment actually permitted a slave to enlist, unofficially of course. After Fort Sumter hundreds of African Americans petitioned the government, and entire companies tried to enroll. The Montgomery delegates heard stories of more than fifteen hundred free blacks who wanted to join in New Orleans. Like other native-born Southerners black Southerners had heard tales of the destruction that would come to their homeland if the enemy invaded. Though some white Southerners certainly saw the reasoning behind these pleas, the fear of armed blacks was too great for the law to change.[1]

Racism existed in the North as well, but President Abraham Lincoln understood the value of undermining the Southern social system and, when he thought the time was right, would call for the enlistment of black soldiers. Of the 180,000 African Americans who served in the Northern armies, the majority were ex-slaves. An estimated 21,667 free blacks were of military age, while some 668,956 male slaves were of military age. Southerners did not see this population of well over half a million as a military asset; in fact, the thought of arming a black man brought out deeply seated anxieties born of the fear of slave rebellions. Southern slaves were used in the war effort just as they had been used during peacetime, as laborers and servants. They dug fortifications, drove wagons, cooked, cleaned, and washed clothes for white soldiers, but they did not fight. During the war a few liberal Confederates suggested that using blacks in combat roles was a viable option, but this idea did not garner much support. Not until the end was in sight and the Confederacy on the road to defeat did policy change.[2]

There were exceptions. Soon after the war began, free blacks in New Orleans organized into the Native Guards, and on May 2 Louisiana's governor allowed the unit to join the state militia. The Louisiana Native Guards had a white commander, but the rest of the officers were black, and a local newspaper reported this unit would "fight the Black Republican with as much determination and gallantry as any body of white men in the service of the Confederate States." These recruits were not your average house servant or field hand, however; these men were from the New Orleans black elite, and many had white ancestors. Together they claimed more than two million dollars in property; each officer had a net worth of more than twenty-five thousand dollars. Some of these wealthy blacks even owned slaves.[3]

By January 1862 the Louisiana Native Guards comprised slightly more than nine hundred men organized into thirteen companies. Yet these new soldiers could not escape the spreading poison of racism and became increasingly unhappy with their treatment; members began disappearing without leave. Moreover, in February, after white citizens complained about the presence of armed blacks, the governor disbanded the Guards, only to recall them in late March when the city's safety appeared threatened. When New Orleans fell in April 1862, some of the black soldiers fled north with the retreating Confederates but were told that the Confederate government would not allow African Americans to join the Southern armies. Many men returned to New Orleans where, under Major General Benjamin F.

Butler, they rejoined the military—this time in Union blue. Just days after Abraham Lincoln announced his Emancipation Proclamation in September 1862, Butler mustered the First Regiment of the Native Guards into the U.S. Army. One authority states that only 11 percent of the pro-Confederate members joined the Union unit, some 108 men. Butler used former slaves emancipated off the plantations in southern Louisiana as volunteers instead. He organized the Second Native Guards in October and the Third Native Guards in November. When Nathaniel P. Banks took command of Union-occupied New Orleans, he relegated the black regiments to garrison duty in remote places where they would not come in contact with white soldiers, for white Union soldiers showed no desire to serve alongside blacks. One of those garrison posts was Port Hudson in Louisiana, where, in May 1863, black soldiers participated in their first major battle.[4]

The question of African Americans as soldiers was not only controversial for both sides, it was actually divisive. Confederates, of course, had to deal with the prospect of seeing their former slaves in uniform. But seeing blacks in Union blue was one thing; having them wear Confederate gray was quite another. During the months when the Confederate Army of Tennessee wintered at Dalton in late 1863, Major General Patrick R. Cleburne drafted a proposal to enlist slaves in the Confederate army in exchange for freedom. He believed enrolling blacks would increase the number of eligible fighting men at a time when desertion was high and would eliminate the slavery issue that kept England and France from recognizing the Southern nation. Irish by birth and Arkansan by choice, Cleburne suggested arming some three hundred thousand slaves; he believed a black man would fight for the South if offered emancipation.[5]

Not only would Cleburne suggest freeing the slaves, but also his plan would have liberated their wives and children, sanctified marriages, and given legal status to their paternity. Cleburne went so far as to suggest that it might be necessary to "emancipate the whole race." Such a radical proposal provoked heated debate among the commanders within the Confederate Army of Tennessee. Mississippian William Bate responded immediately that Cleburne's idea was "hideous and objectionable," the "serpent of Abolitionism." Tennessee-born Patton Anderson, who had enlisted in the Deep South, called it a "Monstrous proposition" that was "revolting to Southern sentiment, Southern pride, and Southern honor." Georgian William H. T. Walker was perhaps the most critical; he called the plan treason. All the opponents insisted that enlisting blacks as soldiers in the Rebel army would cause white soldiers to quit in disgust, as such an idea challenged the very fabric of Southern society.[6]

So sensitive was the subject that after a private meeting General Joseph E. Johnston ordered his commanders not to discuss it and, in particular, to keep the suggestion from reaching the men in the ranks. Walker, however, was not willing to end the discussion there. He asked Cleburne for a copy of the "incendiary" proposal, which the Irishman happily gave him, and he sent the document to President Davis by special messenger. Walker's excuse for disobeying Johnston's instructions was that he believed that the suggestion was too serious to disregard with a mere slap on the hand. He felt that using blacks in combat roles would "involve our cause in ruin and disgrace" and that Cleburne had gone too far. But the president had too many problems as 1864 opened to want another, particularly a controversial issue involving slavery, and he told Walker to ignore the recommendation. At that time Davis believed any other course could cause a revolution within the South.[7]

This footnote to history was almost lost following the war. Because of the nature of Cleburne's proposal, President Davis ordered all the copies destroyed. Cleburne fell at the Battle of Franklin in November 1864, and few remembered his controversial proposal after his death. Not until the death of Major Calhoun Benham some two decades later did a copy surface. Benham had been so upset with the paper that he had requested a copy from Cleburne so that he could prepare a rebuttal; that copy was the only one to survive. Still, not until 1898, when Walker's correspondence became public, would the entire story come to light.[8]

To believe that armed blacks would have been tolerated in the Confederate army challenges the racism of the time. Racism was strong in both North and South, and African Americans were at the top of a long list that included Irish Catholics and other undesirable foreigners. Southern soldiers loathed the idea of fighting former slaves, black men now armed with weapons denied them before the war. One incident that occurred in Georgia exemplifies the typical Rebel reaction.

When John Bell Hood's army approached a Federal supply depot at Dalton in October 1864, white Confederates with the Army of Tennessee faced their first prospect of a battle involving blacks in Union blue. Hood warned the Union commander that he could offer paroles for all white officers and soldiers but that, if he had to assault Dalton, he would take no prisoners. An Indiana soldier claimed this meant that "all Dark soldiers would be shott or Hung." It was well known by that time that blacks had not received fair treatment in a number of skirmishes along the Mississippi River.[9]

After the Union colonel declined to surrender the garrison, Hood talked to him under a flag of truce. Casualties had already occurred, and Hood warned that "he could not restrain his men, and would not if he could." The colonel believed the Rebel soldiers would massacre the black enlisted men, for he had heard the Rebels taunting the black troops and their white officers with threats such as "Kill every damn one of them." Nonetheless, once he realized he had no other option, the colonel gave up after receiving assurances that the black enlisted men would be "treated humanely."[10]

Few African Americans really expected humane treatment. A white lieutenant in the Forty-fourth United States Colored Troops recalled: "As soon as the terms of surrender were made known my men flocked around me and asked if I thought their lives would be spared or [if] they would be murdered as some they knew at Fort Pillow [the previous April]. Of course I could not answer them positively but quieted their fears as much as possible." When the white officers asked to stay with their men to see that the Rebels upheld their part of the bargain, Hood refused and told the colonel that the black captives were not prisoners of war; he considered them as runaway slaves and they would be restored to their owners.[11]

True to his word, Hood returned the blacks to bondage. He turned over around six hundred blacks to individuals claiming to be their owners, but about half ended up in Mississippi. A Charleston newspaper reported, "The negro soldiers were at once divested of their blankets, overcoats, shoes, hats, and in many cases, their breeches." After the captives were stripped, they were put to work tearing up the railroad. When an African American sergeant complained, an Arkansas soldier recalled that "he paid the penalty for disobeying orders"—probably meaning he was shot—and "the rest tore up the road readily." Another man "was shot on the spot, as were also five others shortly after surrender, who, having been sick, were unable to keep up with the rest on the march."[12]

In his explanation of the Dalton incident to the commander of black troops at Nashville, the Union colonel stated that the Rebels robbed and abused the prisoners in a "terrible manner." He singled out General Bate, the same Mississippian who so vehemently opposed Cleburne's proposal to arm slaves, for his "meanness and beastly conduct." A Cincinnati newspaper called Bate a "brute" and claimed that he wanted to "dispose" of (meaning execute) any man who willingly commanded African American soldiers.[13]

It is impossible to trace the fate of the captured African Americans, although some were still prisoners several weeks later. A Southerner who saw them in Alabama noted that the majority of the captives were very young and said that a "man with any humanity could not look upon them with any other than feelings of the deepest pity." General P. G. T. Beauregard officially inquired about the condition of the prisoners when he asked whether the blacks working on the railroad and fortifications around Corinth, Mississippi, were the same ones captured in Georgia. A Charleston newspaper declared, "As a general thing, the men of the army were in favor of hanging the last one of them on the nearest limbs," and it was "very questionable" whether many survived long as prisoners of war.[14]

The treatment of black prisoners was similar in almost every battle involving black soldiers. In some encounters the results were even more violent, with few blacks surviving. This intense racism makes questionable whether most Confederates would have tolerated armed blacks in their own ranks, and as noble as Cleburne's proposal might sound to us today, it was extremely naive for the time. Most Rebel soldiers, products of an environment based on two centuries of slavery, did not want to see blacks in Confederate gray anymore than they wanted to face blacks in Union blue. An armed black man was a danger to society as Southerners understood it; thus, Cleburne's proposal to enlist blacks as soldiers frightened his fellow officers, who saw it as an attack on the core of the Southern system. Moreover, it usurped planters' property, and that tore at the foundation of Southern democracy. Georgian Howell Cobb insisted: "The day you make soldiers of them is the beginning of the end of the revolution. If slaves will make good soldiers, our whole theory of slavery is wrong."[15]

Certainly blacks served unofficially in numerous cases. One Jacob Jones, a slave, for example, had his name on the rolls of the Ninth Virginia as a musician. Similarly, a man known only as "Joe" was a soldier-teamster in the Thirteenth Virginia. But no matter a black soldier's unofficial capacities, a black man armed with a weapon was not typical.

Instead, Confederate commanders urged using slaves for menial jobs to release more white soldiers for frontline duty. This suggestion took root, and various commanders impressed slaves to drive wagons, dig earthworks, and tend livestock. General Johnston, for instance, used slaves as teamsters and cooks and sent the white soldiers who had been doing these jobs to the front. A slave working for the army in the same role he had held in bondage was not a danger, and few objections surfaced. One obvious reason for using blacks in the military was the abundance of male slaves on the plantations without proper supervision. Men worried about their wives and children as the number of competent overseers decreased and slaves began to outnumber able-bodied white men on the home front. To lessen the threat to civilians everyone agreed that sending male slaves off to the military was a good idea. To do so not only worked as a form of social control but also addressed the dwindling ranks in the Confederate army. None of these slaves received freedom in exchange for military service, and none carried a weapon. One Southerner accurately noted, "If we fail to swell our ranks with the slaves, the foe wil most surely swell his ranks with the slaves."[16]

This was a succinct assessment of Lincoln's intentions. While Southerners debated about how to deal with blacks in the South, the decision to enlist freed slaves in Northern armies slowly gained support. Before the fighting ended, black soldiers in Union blue had fought in almost 450 engagements, although most were too small to even rate a name. By the last year of the war they were serving in the main Union army in Virginia under George G. Meade and Ulysses S. Grant and in the Union army in Tennessee under George Thomas. They fought at Nashville, the battle that destroyed the Confederate Army of Tennessee in December 1864. Together Thomas, Grant, and William T. Sherman led the principal armies that would win the war by 1865. Sherman, however, did not welcome blacks into his ranks, and his resistance is a reflection of the feelings of many Union soldiers. The 1989 film *Glory* introduced the public to African American soldiers in the U.S. Army, but the movie also emphasized that, although blacks made a significant contribution to the war effort, they also faced a bitter fight for acceptance from Northern white soldiers.

When Lincoln's Emancipation Proclamation went into effect on Thursday, January 1, 1863, it included a paragraph not in the original document. Not only would slaves in most of the Confederate States be freed but blacks would "be received into the armed service of the United States to garrison forts, positions, stations, and other places, and to man vessels of all sort in said service." By this time some African American units were already serving unofficially in the military, but this statement made the enlistment of blacks, including Southern blacks, official policy. By the end of the war African Americans filled 133 infantry regiments, 4 independent companies, 7 cavalry regiments, 12 regiments of heavy artillery, and 10 companies of light artillery. Some 57 percent came from the eleven Confederate States and 24 percent from the border states of Missouri, Kentucky, Maryland, and Delaware.[17]

This was a new direction for the government in Washington. Although blacks had fought in the American war for independence, a law in 1792 had prohibited them from joining state militias or enlisting in the U.S. Army. Northerners, just as much as Southerners, objected to an armed black man in the years before the war. Even after the Civil War began, Lincoln had turned away free black volunteers for fear of reaction among his constituents. Although Lincoln had changed his direction by 1862, strong resistance to freeing and arming ex-slaves still existed. But as the war continued with no end in sight, even opponents of blacks in the Northern ranks could see the logic of filling the regiments with men who could prevent the further sacrifice of Northern white soldiers. When the North turned to a draft, this logic became even more apparent. Moreover, as the number of black refugees in Union-occupied regions swelled, Lincoln needed a way to employ the freed slaves productively.[18]

Lincoln's initial objections to arming blacks had come from sound practical reasoning. When the state of Indiana offered to recruit two regiments of blacks in August 1862, Lincoln responded by saying that "the nation could not afford to lose Kentucky at this crisis, and . . . that to arm the negroes would turn 50,000 bayonets from the loyal Border States against us that were for us." Yet some radical abolitionists had their own agenda. After Fort Pulaski, near Savannah, fell in April 1862, for example, General David Hunter liberated the slaves and used them as laborers without the permission of the War Department. He then freed the slaves along a thin stretch of coastal Georgia, South Carolina, and Florida and enlisted all able-bodied blacks between eighteen and forty-five. Even after Lincoln told Hunter to stop, the general continued to liberate and recruit slaves from coastal plantations. Although a critic of Hunter's tactics noted that his harsh methods were "valuable as an example of how not to do it," many radical abolitionists applauded his actions. By October the first regiment of former slaves to receive official recognition from the War Department began to organize; this regiment became the First South Carolina Volunteers.[19]

Although other black regiments followed in South Carolina, the majority of freed slaves who joined the Union army came from the Confederate heartland and along the Mississippi River. In March 1863 Lorenzo Thomas arrived in the Mississippi Valley with instructions to recruit blacks and by May had enlisted his first unit, the First Arkansas Volunteers of African Descent. By the end of 1863 he had filled twenty black regiments, and by the end of the war he had added another fifty. Fully 40 percent of the African American regiments came from Thomas's hard work in the Mississippi River valley.[20]

Like Rebel soldiers, most Confederate civilians had strong feelings about Southern blacks who wore Union blue. The first time that George Richard Browder, a Methodist preacher in south-central Kentucky, saw armed blacks, he declared, "The sight was very revolting to me & other Kentuckians." President Jefferson Davis called the Emancipation Proclamation "the most execrable measure recorded in the history of guilty man" and announced that "all negro slaves captured in arms" and their white officers would be tried. The Reverend Browder later noted that "confederates hang or shoot all the negroes they find in uniform & say they will give all the officers captured since the issuing of Lincolns proclamation into the hands of the State authorities to be punished for exciting insurrection. The penalty is death & this may lead to cruel & bloody retaliation." The results were predictable. Atrocities occurred at the battles of Port Hudson (May 27), Milliken's Bend (June 7), and Mound Plantation (June 29) in Louisiana, and at the Battle of Battery Wagner (July 18) in South Carolina, all in 1863. Port Hudson, Milliken's Bend, and Battery Wagner were the first times the U.S. Army officially used blacks in combat roles.[21]

Pension records reveal some of the travails of Southern blacks in Union blue. Obviously they had a strong fear of being murdered by Confederate soldiers, so being returned to slavery seemed a preferable alternative. Private Adam Cook of the Forty-sixth Unites States Colored Troops recalled the concern of Confederate brigadier general James C. Tappan, who commanded Arkansas troops, after his capture at Mound Plantation. "If it had not been for him we would have been killed," the black soldier claimed. "There were some Texas Rangers about, and they would as soon kill one of us as to eat. We did not belong to them and they did not care how many they killed. I was struck three or four times by them for not keeping up." Another black soldier, Charles Bogan, recalled, "We were threatened with hanging & killing every minute & we were pretty badly scared." One Edward Terry recalled that after the Rebel attack on Mound Plantation he was turned over to a white man named Ben Chandler who carried him back to Texas where he remained in bondage until the end of the war. When he later applied for a military pension, he was turned down because he was considered a deserter.[22]

The stories varied, but the results were the same. Samuel Anderson, who had been born at Key West, Florida, around 1838, was also captured by the Texas cavalry in Louisiana. In a deposition in 1896, he recalled: "Capt. Ingraham who was one of the officers who took us prisoners took me as a body servant, and took me with him to Hill Co., Texas. . . . He left me there until 1867 when I ran away and came to N.O. [New Orleans]." Although it is unlikely he remained in bondage for two years following the war, the gist of his story is certainly true. George W. Ingram was a lieutenant in Company C, Twelfth Texas Cavalry, at the time of the fight at Mound Plantation but was promoted to captain in the spring of 1864. He may have kept Anderson with him in camp, or he many have taken him to his home in Texas before the war ended. In spite of laws condemning such action, most Texans disregarded them. In February 1864 Ingram wrote his wife: "I have a Negro boy that I will take or send home to herd our horses in the Spring. He is a very sprightly boy about 14 or 15 years old." This story is typical of what happened to Southern blacks in the Trans-Mississippi and western theaters. Most Texans agreed with what a Mississippi Rebel wrote his mother: "I hope I may never see a Negro soldier . . . or I cannot be . . . a Christian soldier."[23]

The problems associated with blacks captured in northern Louisiana became so troublesome that one colonel had to issue orders prohibiting his men from keeping or selling property taken when raiding. He pointed out that property such as horses, mules, and former slaves belonged to the Confederate government and any "disposed of or used without the consent of Brigade or Regimental Commander will be regarded as a crime and severely punished." When twenty-year-old James Callahan was found guilty of stealing a mule, he was "dishonorably dismounted as no longer worthy to be a member of the cavalry arm of the Confederate army." His punishment was transfer to the infantry. Although no indication exists that this was the punishment for retaining or selling black captives and the colonel admitted he was "pained to take this course," he still felt he had to take drastic measures. Nonetheless, it is more likely he gave permission for officers to keep captured blacks for use as body servants.[24]

The treatment of Southern blacks in Union blue finally forced Lincoln to issue the following statement in July 1863: "To sell or enslave any captured person on account of his color and for no offense against the laws of war is a relapse into barbarism and a crime against the civilization of the age." He continued by warning that "for every soldier of the United States killed in violation of the laws of war a rebel soldier shall be executed, and for every one enslaved by the enemy or sold into slavery a rebel soldier shall be placed at hard labor . . . until the other shall be released and receive the treatment due to a prisoner of war." Lincoln's words had no effect on the average Confederate soldier, particularly in the Mississippi Valley and Trans-Mississippi. Stories of brutality continued; there were claims of atrocities committed by Nathan Bedford Forrest's troops at Fort Pillow and by Confederate soldiers in the fighting at Poison Spring, Arkansas, both in 1864.[25]

One vocal opponent to the Union policy of arming Southern blacks was Ohio-born William Tecumseh Sherman. In fact, Northerners were as likely to oppose enlisting blacks in Northern armies as Southerners were to object to facing their former slaves. "I prefer some negroes as pioneers, teamsters, cooks, and servants," Sherman declared in July 1864, "others gradually to experiment in the art of the Soldier, beginning with the duties of local garrison such as we had at Memphis, Vicksburg, Natchez—Nashville and Chattanooga." Sherman's first experience with black troops had come in the spring of 1863 when he was a major general under Ulysses S. Grant during the final months of the Vicksburg campaign. As Union armies moved down the Mississippi River, the number of African Americans coming into Union lines increased, and the burden on the quartermaster department grew. From Helena, Arkansas, Colonel Cyrus Bussey observed: "There are a great many Negro men, women and children coming into our lines since the proclamation; many are leaving their homes. I am at a loss to know what to do with them." Similarly, Major General Samuel R. Curtis had observed from Saint Louis that blacks arrived by the boat loads, and his department already had "more of these, unfortunately," than he knew "what to do with." If the able-bodied males were used at all, they filled the traditional roles of laborers or servants.[26]

Grant soon received instructions from General-in-Chief Henry Halleck that the policy toward escaped slaves was to change. Because the new plan involved using Southern blacks against Southern whites, Grant assured Halleck that he would "take hold of the new policy of arming negroes and using them against the rebels with a will." One change involved the designations of black regiments. No longer would the regiments carry the state of origin in their names; instead, they became United States Colored Troops or simply USCT. Only a few black units received permission to retain their original affiliations, and these were generally the well-known ones like the Fifty-fourth and Fifty-fifth Massachusetts, which included educated free blacks from the Northeast. No change occurred in the officer corps, however, as the commissioned officers typically continued to be white.[27]

By March 1863 the War Department had created the Bureau for Colored Troops attached to the adjutant general's office and five months later had accepted some fifty-eight regiments of African Americans. By December the bureau reported that 20,830 black males had enlisted in various regiments in the Mississippi Valley. Although Lincoln could clearly revel in his success, not all Union soldiers agreed with the administration's new policy. Many Union soldiers from the Midwest could have easily rivaled Southern soldiers in their abhorrence of an armed black. Sherman, who became commander of the

Military Division of the Mississippi, remained a strong opponent of using blacks in any roles other than traditional ones closely resembling those they had as slaves.[28]

Although Sherman held strong opinions about the status of blacks in a white society, he also understood what integrating the army would mean to his men. Few in the Union armies in the western theater were abolitionists, and Lincoln's Emancipation Proclamation had not enjoyed much support. Sherman understood the temper of his troops when he noted that the "great mass of [U.S.] soldiery must be of the white race, and the black troops should for some years be used with caution." He refused to carry out a policy that he thought upset the natural order and argued that he should not be forced. "For God's sake," he added, "let the negro question develop itself slowly and naturally, and not by premature cultivation make it a weak element in our policy."[29]

Because Sherman commanded the Union armies in the Confederate heartland in 1864, the first full year of active recruiting, his attitude was a problem for the administration. Secretary of War Edwin Stanton told Lorenzo Thomas, "General Sherman seems to think that the colored troops reported to be raised by you on the Mississippi are chiefly on paper, and that the men are not to be found." Indeed, nothing would have pleased Sherman more than to lose the men Thomas had recruited in a stack of paperwork. Sherman confided to his wife that, although he was willing to treat former slaves "as free," he did not think they should be "hunted & badgered to make a soldier of when his family is left back on the Plantations." Clearly he thought Thomas was wrong in going among the black refugees to enroll soldiers, and Sherman told his wife, "I am right & Wont Change."[30]

"I think I understand the negro as well as anybody," Sherman claimed in defending his position. A freedman "must pass through a probationary state," Sherman stated, before he would be ready for "utter and complete freedom." Sherman did agree to use Southern blacks as teamsters, pioneers, or servants and by early 1864 had "no objection to the surplus, if any, being enlisted as soldiers." He had no intention of having any surplus, though, because he would always find reasons why he needed more teamsters, pioneers, and servants. "I must have labor and a large quantity of it," he observed. "I confess I would prefer 300 negroes armed with spades and axes than 1,000 as soldiers." He also told a recruiter, "I would not draw on the Poor race for too large a proportion of its active athletic young men, for some must remain to seek new homes, and provide for the old and young, the feeble and helpless."[31]

Sherman's point of view came from years of living in the Southern states, and he prided himself on his knowledge of the region. Because of his experiences, reaching from South Carolina to Louisiana, he believed that he understood his subjects better than anyone in Washington. He had been a resident of Louisiana when the state seceded and had lived in the South, off and on, for more than twenty years. In October 1859 Sherman had accepted a position as superintendent of a new state school near Alexandria, today's Louisiana State University. Although he was Northern born and, as one of the men who voted against the appointment pointed out, "the son-in-law of that blackhearted Abolitionist [senator] Tom Ewing," he fit in well in his Southern surroundings. He believed in the inferiority of slaves, thought slavery a sensible form of social control, and even wrote that the "relations between master and slave [could] not be changed without utter ruin to immense numbers," and he was "not sure that the slave would be benefitted thereby." In fact, he had even told his wife, Ellen, that, if she moved south to live with him in Louisiana, she would probably have to buy a slave because free labor did not exist and he knew she required several servants.[32]

Sherman argued that his position was shared "by a large portion" of Northern soldiers. In the spring of 1863 Sherman had told his wife: "I would prefer to have this a white man's war and provide for the negroes after the time has passed. . . . With my opinion of negroes and my experience, yea prejudice, I cannot trust them yet." Writing to his brother nine days later, he repeated, "I won't trust [blacks] to fight yet."[33]

He particularly disliked recruiters following his army. Typically recruiters filled their quotas by tracking victorious Union armies through the South. Slaves flocked to the promise of freedom when they heard of the passage of Northern columns, providing a willing source of manpower. To counter the recruiters, in June 1864 Sherman issued an order stating that recruiting officers could not "enlist as soldiers any negroes who are profitably employed" by the army. He added that any recruiter who interfered with blacks working for the army could be arrested and imprisoned.[34]

Sherman never wavered; he objected to the use of slaves as combat soldiers with long letters directed at anyone who would listen. While, on the one hand, Sherman admitted that the use of black soldiers was an "open question" that "should be fairly and honestly tested," on the other, he would do his best to keep them out of his own fighting forces by relegating them to noncombat duty. He insisted that he had "no objection to the enlistment of negroes if [his] working parties [were] not interfered with," but, he added, "If they are interfered with I must put a summary stop to it." He also thought recruiting in north Georgia was "a waste of time," as blacks were "as scarce in North Georgia as in Ohio." He claimed he had not "seen an able bodied man black or white there fit for a soldier who was not in this Army or the one opposed to it."[35]

Recruiting black soldiers in the Confederate heartland did not progress as easily as it did in the Mississippi River valley. The political power of slaveholders in Tennessee who professed loyalty to the Union prevented dipping into slave reserves, and because recruiters operated out of Nashville, they met resistance at every turn. Not until late 1863 did Boston businessman George L. Stearns (who had organized the Fifty-fourth and Fifty-fifth Massachusetts) arrive in the state capital. Using money raised by Massachusetts abolitionists, he enlisted six regiments before resigning. In October the *Nashville Daily Press* reported, "Our citizens yesterday saw, for the first time, a regiment of colored troops marching through the streets of Nashville," but "the novelty of armed negro troops elicited many remarks about the policy of the Administration in raising them—both *pro and con*."[36]

Stearns's chief assistant, Reuben D. Mussey of the Nineteenth U.S. Infantry, carried on the work when he became the commissioner for the organization of black units in middle and east Tennessee in February. That same month a local paper reported: "Tennessee has furnished 30,000 white troops to the Union Army, she has given equally as good a report of herself in regard to the formation of colored troops. Already upwards of twelve thousand colored troops have been enlisted." Although many did not support the efforts to arm blacks—including, initially, Union governor Andrew Johnson—as the number of contrabands (as former slaves were called) grew, recruiting centers appeared at Murfreesboro, Clarksville, Gallatin, and Shelbyville. The same problem had emerged in Tennessee that had plagued Union commanders in the Mississippi River valley. They had thousands of mouths to feed and protect; enlisting the able-bodied men reduced some of the strain on resources.[37]

What is known about Southern blacks in Northern armies comes from records kept by the recruiters or from letters and diaries of the white officers who served in the regiments. Very few slaves could read or write, for the field hands who made up most of the Northern ranks had had no chance for an education. Michigan native Morris S. Hall, who became officer in the Forty-fourth USCT, recalled the difficulties involved. The Forty-fourth consisted of former slaves from northwest Georgia. In his reminiscences he described the challenge he faced:

> Of the 86 men mustered in . . . only 9 could read and write and 23 knew their letters. I at once sent home for primers, spelling and reading books and writing material and little Testaments, and commenced an effort to educate them, and I am proud of the result. Of 148 men all told who were taken into that company [during the Forty-fourth's two years of service] not one remained to be mustered out who could not read and write and spell, and many of them became good mathematicians, good in geography and even grammar. In all of my experience here at the north I never saw such progress. I began by teaching a class of the more apt ones and made them the teachers of the others. After the readers and spelling books came each

one was provided with one of each, or a primer when they did not know their letters; and as they went on duty you would see a book tucked under the belt, and as soon as a tour of duty was through they would spread a poncho or blanket on the ground and fill the time full of study, trying as far as possible to learn by themselves.[38]

The former slaves also made motivated combat soldiers. An officer in the Twelfth USCT observed, "From slavery to freedom was itself a grand transition; but to become Union soldiers was a still bigger promotion, exceeding their most sanguine hopes—a privilege estimated at its full value." An officer in the Thirteenth USCT noted that the troops were "the bravest set of men on the Western Continent. They think nothing of routing the guerrillas, that roam at large in the wilds of Tennessee." Colonel Thomas J. Morgan, who commanded the First Colored Brigade in the Battle of Nashville in December 1864, likewise believed black soldiers made good fighting men. When organizing the Fourteenth USCT in late 1863, he had interviewed each recruit personally. "When I told . . . one who wanted to 'fight for freedom,' that he might lose his life," Morgan recalled, the man replied, "But my people will be free."[39]

During the Battle of Nashville, men from the 12th, 13th, and 100th USCT took part in a suicidal frontal assault. As soon as they received the assignment, they knew it would be difficult, for the attack on heavily fortified Rebel soldiers would be over a plowed field, and mud would hamper their forward progress. In preparation, some soldiers asked their white officers to hold their money or valuables. "This and little talk among themselves showed a settled resolution, to unflinchingly face death in the cause of freedom and nationality," commented Captain D. E. Straight of the 100th USCT.[40]

The attack impressed the Rebel soldiers. "On they came in splendid order," a Rebel artilleryman recalled from his fortified position. When men in the 100th and 12th USCT faltered, soldiers from the 13th struggled on even though this was their first time under fire. "There were very few negroes who retreated in our front," declared an Alabamian, "and none were at their post when the firing ceased; for we fired as long as there was anything to shoot at." A Union surgeon who treated the wounded told his family: "Don't tell me negroes won't fight! I know better." The 13th USCT suffered 220 casualties in its first battle, nearly 40 percent of the regiment's strength.[41]

Although blacks fought at Nashville in December 1864, Sherman had resisted all efforts to integrate his white armies moving on Atlanta in the summer. In July he had informed a recruiter that, although he felt he was a friend of the black man, he would not change his decision to use them exclusively in such traditional roles as cooks and servants. He lectured a recruiter, telling him that blacks were "in a transition state" and were therefore "not the equal of the white man." Moreover, it was "unjust" to the white soldiers in his army "to place them on a *par*" with black recruits.[42]

By this time Sherman had critics in powerful circles. Reuben Mussey forwarded Sherman's letter up the line along with one of his own that criticized the general. Mussey believed that Sherman was "fully two years behind the time" in his attitude toward slavery. Although Mussey was too smart to challenge Sherman publicly, he added, "And when I say two years I mean two of those century like years which we are living."[43]

Apparently Sherman wanted his views to go public even though he told a friend that he "thought it would never get into the press." Although Sherman pretended to abhor politics, in reality he was extremely political and understood exactly where his letter would end up—in newspapers nationwide. He played on the racism of most Northerners when he said that he liked blacks if they remained in their place, "but when fools and idiots [meaning white recruiters] try to make [them] better than ourselves, I have an opinion." He had even told Halleck that a black man might be as good as a white man to stop a bullet, but "a sand-bag is better." Could they skirmish, do picket duty, and improvise when necessary? he asked. "I say no," he answered rhetorically. Back in June, Lorenzo Thomas had written Sherman about the subject on behalf of the secretary of war. "I have seen your recent order respecting the enlistment of negroes," Thomas observed of Sherman's threat to arrest recruiters, and it will "almost altogether stop recruiting with your army. I don't know under what circumstances it was issued, but the imprisonment of officers for disobedience seems to me a harsh measure." Two days later Thomas pointed out that blacks were coming in to join "very rapidly," and he needed the general's cooperation. Lincoln reminded Sherman that the law regarding black recruitment was "a law" and "must be treated as such by all." More to the point, Lincoln concluded, "May I ask therefore that you will give your hearty co-operation?"[44]

Sherman was one of the few individuals to challenge the president on the issue of arming slaves. He informed Lincoln, "I have the highest veneration for the law, and will respect it always, however it conflicts with my opinion of its propriety." Although he admitted that he had "peculiar notions" on the subject of slavery, he could "assure" the president that those notions were "shared" by many soldiers. Sherman's capture of Atlanta made him a Northern hero and strengthened his position in the argument. He labeled recruiters "unscrupulous State agents" and concluded that enlisting soldiers in the occupied South was the "height of folly." In the end Sherman avoided having black units attached to his army in any meaningful role until after Savannah surrendered. At that time he did accept a black regiment, the 110th USCT. True to his word, he ordered the men disarmed and put them to work as laborers, teamsters, and servants. Reports even surfaced that some were killed by white troops. One Ohio soldier judged that the blacks needed to be "taught to know their places & behave civilly." Halleck bluntly told the general that, if the behavior continued, he would have trouble with Washington. Sherman's attitude toward African American soldiers never changed, but the black men in Union blue accompanied the army on its march through South Carolina.[45]

Clearly the road to freedom for Southern blacks was not easy in either the North or the South. In one of history's great ironies Northerners such as Sherman threw obstacles in the road for Southern blacks while forward-thinking Southerners like Patrick Cleburne advocated freedom. Cleburne, in fact, had no way to know that he had scored a victory in the debate over the issue of enlisting blacks in the

Confederate army. Although the public knew nothing of Cleburne's proposal, if the Irishman read any local papers in the autumn of 1864, he would have seen President Davis's tentative suggestion to use slaves in the army. When the last session of the Confederate Congress convened on November 7, Davis, although still personally against arming blacks, declared, "Should the alternative ever be presented of subjugation or of the employment of the slave as a soldier, there seems to be no reason to doubt what should then be our decision."[46]

The idea of arming blacks had little support in the Confederacy to the last. Even after Davis suggested using slaves in menial jobs, the *Daily Examiner* in Richmond challenged that enlisting African Americans was a "confession, not only of weakness, but of absolute inability to secure the object for which we undertook the war." The fighting ended before the controversial law that would issue muskets to Southern slaves became a reality in practice.[47]

Although blacks in Confederate gray were rare, those in Union blue served with distinction, and more than one-third, or 68,178, died. Yet only 2,751 were killed in action; the rest were reported missing or died from disease or wounds. A surgeon assigned to the USCT in 1863 noted, "Very few surgeons will do precisely the same for blacks as they would for whites," and a white officer from Louisiana added, "The mortality in our Regt. beats anything I ever saw." Even Lorenzo Thomas observed, when seeing the filth in a USCT hospital in Nashville, that, if these men had been white soldiers, "think you this would have been their condition? No!"[48]

African Americans fought in every theater of the war from the Rio Grande to Virginia. They even took part in battles before the Emancipation Proclamation went into effect—a skirmish in Missouri in October 1862 involving the First Kansas Volunteers (Colored). African American soldiers generally acquitted themselves well in each battle in which they participated, from 1862 until the fight at Palmetto Ranch, the last battle of the Civil War on May 11 and 12, 1865, a skirmish involving the Sixty-second USCT on the Rio Grande border between Texas and Mexico.[49]

Perhaps the contribution of black soldiers is best recalled by one of the white officers who led them in battle, Morris S. Hall, who wrote in his reminiscences how he parted from his "brave boys," former slaves from northwest Georgia, upon the disbanding of the Forty-fourth USCT in Nashville in 1866:

> [W]e served without pay from April 30 to May 5th and kept order there while all the other troops mustered out. Our equipment was then turned over to the quarter and ordinance officers and we drew our pay and were declared to be free men and citizens of the U.S. instead of sol-diers. I had a strong desire to bid the men good bye in a way that they would carry my good wishes and a parting blessing and instruction and advice for their future life as citizens. So I asked them all to march back to our company quarters and remain in ranks while I addressed them. It seemed to me then that I was inspired in this address of 15 or 20 minutes, and when I took their hands to say good bye to each one personally there was not a dry eye in the company. Many could not speak for emotion but would point to heaven, others said, "God bless you, Captain, we will meet you on the other shore." So I trust I shall meet many of them there, and I am sure I shall recognize them too.[50]

NOTES

ONE. BROKEN PROMISES

1. Roger L. Ransom, "Population," in *Encyclopedia of the Confederacy*, ed. Richard N. Current, 4 vols. (New York: Simon and Schuster, 1993), 3:1233–35; Jason H. Silverman, "Foreigners," in ibid., 2:602–4; Jason H. Silverman, "Germans," in ibid., 2:675–76. See also Rudolph L. Biesele, *The History of the German Settlements in Texas, 1833–1861* (Austin: n.p., 1930); George Charles Engerrand, *The So-called Wends of Germany and Their Colonies in Texas and in Australia* (Austin: University of Texas Bureau of Research in the Social Sciences, [1934]); Glen E. Lich and Dona B. Reeves, eds., *German Culture in Texas* (Boston: Twayne, 1980); and Glen E. Lich, *The German Texans* (San Antonio: University of Texas Institute of Texan Cultures, 1981).

2. One of the best surveys of German immigrants is Randall M. Miller, "Germans," in *Encyclopedia of Southern Culture*, ed. Charles Reagan Wilson and William Ferris (Chapel Hill: University of North Carolina Press, 1989), 429–31. Miller also wrote about Germans in the urban South in "The Enemy Within: Some Effects of Foreign Immigrants on Antebellum Southern Cities," *Southern Studies* 34 (Spring 1985): 30–53.

3. Joseph R. Reinhart, ed. and trans., *Two Germans in the Civil War: The Diary of John Daeuble and the Letters of Gottfried Rentschler, 6th Kentucky Volunteer Infantry* (Knoxville: University of Tennessee Press, 2004), xix–xxii, 169–70; John C. Inscoe, "Appalachian Otherness, Read and Perceived," in *The New Georgia Guide* (Athens: University of Georgia Press, 1996), 192–93.

4. Grady McWhiney, *Cracker Culture: Celtic Ways in the Old South* (Tuscaloosa: University of Alabama Press, 1988), 2–3, 19–20, 86; Frederick Law Olmsted, *A Journey through Texas; or, a Saddle-Trip on the Southwestern Frontier* (New York: Dix, Edwards and Co., 1857), 140–47, 149, 167, 178–90. For more on the Celtic heritage of Confederate soldiers, see Grady McWhiney and Perry D. Jamieson, *Attack and Die: Civil War Military Tactics and the Southern Heritage* (Tuscaloosa: University of Alabama Press, 1982), chapter 12.

5. The earliest significant German settlement came under Mexican rule and was financed by Baron von Bastrop in 1823. Information on early German settlements in America is plentiful, although many of the sources are in German. For a sampling, see Franz Löher, *Geschichte und Zustände der Deutschen in Amerika* (Cincinnati: Eggers and Wulkop; Leipzig: K. F. Köhler, 1847); Ottomar von Behr, *Guter Rath für Auswanderer nach den Vereinigten Staaten von Nord*

America mit besonderer Berücksichtigung von Texas . . . (Leipzig: Robert Friese, 1847); Gilbert Giddings Benjamin, *The Germans in Texas* (New York: D. Appleton and Co., 1910); Moritz Beyer, *Das Auswanderungsbuch oder Führer und Rathgeber bei der Auswanderung nach Nord Amerika und Texas* (Leipzig: Baumgartner, 1846); L. Constant, *Texas: Das Verderben deutscher Auswanderer in Texas unter dem Schutze des Mainzer Vereins* (Berlin: Reimer, 1847); Detlef Dunt, *Reise nach Texas, nebst Nachrichten von diesem Lande; für Deutsche, welche nach Amerika zu gehen beabsichtigen* (Bremen: Carl W. Wiehe, 1834); Francis Joseph Grund, *Handbuch und Wegweiser für Auswanderer nach den Vereinigten Staaten von Nordamerika und Texas*, 2nd ed. (Stuttgart: J. G. Cotta, 1846); Caroline von Hinueber, "Life of German Pioneers of Early Texas," *Texas State Historical Association Quarterly* 2 (1899): 227–32; Friedrich Höhne, *Wahn und Ueberzeugung. Reise des Kupferschmiede-Meisters Friedrich Höhne in Weimar über Bremen nach Nordamerika und Texas in den Jahren 1839, 1840 und 1841* (Weimar: Wilhelm Hoffmann, 1844); Heinrich Ostermayer, *Tagebuch einer Reise nach Texas im Jahr 1848–1849* . . . (Biberach: Im Verlage des Verfassers, 1850); J. E. Rabe, *Eine Erholungsfahrt nach Texas und Mexico* . . . (Hamburg: Leopold Voss, 1893); Friedrich Schlecht, *Mein Ausflug nach Texas* (Bunzlau: Appun, 1851); C. Stählen, *Neueste Nachrichten, Erklärungen u. Briefe der Auswanderer von Texas* (Heilbronn: n.p., 1846); Adolf P. Weber, *Deutsche Pioniere: Zur Geschichte des Deutschthums in Texas* (San Antonio: Selbstverlag, 1894); and Moritz Tiling, *History of the German Element in Texas from 1820–1850* (Houston: Rein and Sons, 1913).

6. Terry G. Jordan, "Germans," in *The New Handbook of Texas*, ed. Ron Tyler, 6 vols. (Austin: Texas State Historical Association, 1996), 3:142–44. Ernst was known in Germany as Friedrich Diercks. A professional gardener in the Grand Duchy of Oldenburg in northwestern Germany, he had originally intended to settle in Missouri, where a large German presence was growing in Saint Louis. But on arriving in New Orleans, he learned that land grants were available for foreigners in Texas. He asked for and received four thousand acres, which became the nucleus of the German belt.

7. In 1848 a series of nationalistic and liberal revolutions spread across Europe. Continental liberals wanted more representative governments, civil liberty, and unregulated economic life. When the revolts failed, many liberal Europeans emigrated to America in search of the political and economic freedoms denied them at home. For more on the late arrivals, see A. E. Zucker, ed., *The Forty-eighters: Political Refugees of the German Revolution of 1848* (New York: Columbia University Press, 1950). Historian Terry Jordan warns that it can be misleading to classify the two groups by using the uprisings in 1848. See Terry G. Jordan, *German Seed in Texas Soil: Immigrant Farmers in Nineteenth-Century Texas* (Austin: University of Texas Press, 1966), 182–85. Ella Lonn, in her work on

foreigners in the Confederacy, gives the number of Germans in Texas in 1860 as 20,555. Other historians have estimated more than 30,000. See Ella Lonn, *Foreigners in the Confederacy* (Chapel Hill: University of North Carolina Press, 1940), 31. Jason H. Silverman estimates that roughly 53,000 Germans resided in Texas, Louisiana, and Virginia, and only around 20,000 in the remaining eight Confederate states. Jason H. Silverman, "Germans" and "Irish," in *Encyclopedia of the Confederacy*, 2:675–76, 822–23. The total population of Texas in 1860 was about 604,000, with 183,000 of that number black. Only Florida and Arkansas had fewer African Americans.

8. Olmsted, *A Journey through Texas*, 432.

9. The Second U.S. Cavalry was organized in 1855 with men handpicked by then secretary of war Jefferson Davis, and 710 men left for Texas in October. See Richard W. Johnson, *A Soldier's Reminiscences in Peace and War* (Philadelphia: J. B. Lippincott, 1886), for a personal account of the regiment. See also Harold B. Simpson, *Cry Comanche: The 2nd U.S. Cavalry in Texas, 1855–1861* (Hillsboro, Tex.: Hill Jr. College Press, 1979), for the most complete history and a discussion of fighting Indians on the frontier. Although the Second U.S. Cavalry was organized for service in Texas, it was not the only regiment in the state in 1861. Soldiers frequently visited the German communities along the frontier. At Fredericksburg the register of the Nimitz Hotel carries the signatures of future Confederate general James Longstreet and future Union general Philip Sheridan, and after the turn of the century the proprietor proudly displayed the bed where General Robert E. Lee had slept. See Rena Mazyck Andrews, "German Pioneers in Texas: Civil War Period" (MA thesis, University of Chicago, 1929), 21. For an account of the Indian problems, see J. W. Wilbarger, *Indian Depredations in Texas* (Austin: Hutchings Printing House, 1889); John Henry Brown, *Indian Wars and Pioneers in Texas* (Austin: L. E. Daniell, 1880); and Floyd Ewing, "Origins of Unionist Sentiment on the West Texas Frontier," *West Texas Historical Association Yearbook* 32 (October 1956): 21–29.

10. For a discussion of Texas as southern rather than western in the antebellum days, see Randolph B. Campbell, *Gone to Texas: A History of the Lone Star State* (New York: Oxford University Press, 2003), 207–38. He concludes that "the key to Texas then—and in many respects ever since—lay in its development as an essentially southern state, a part of the south" (206).

11. James I. Robertson Jr., *Soldiers Blue and Gray* (Columbia: University of South Carolina Press, 1988), 100. See also Lonn, *Foreigners in the Confederacy*; and William Kaufman, *The Germans in the American Civil War*, trans. Steven Rowan and ed. Don Heinrich Tolzmann, with Werner D. Mueller and Robert E. Ward (Carlisle, Penn.: John Kallmann, 1999). The latter was originally published in 1911 as *Die Deutschen im Amerikanischen Buergerkrieg*. Ella Lonn, whose

work on foreigners in the Civil War was groundbreaking, died in 1962. Born in LaPorte, Indiana, Lonn graduated from the University of Chicago in 1900 as a Phi Beta Kappa with special honors in history and political science. In spite of the prejudices against women in academics at the time, she completed a PhD at the University of Pennsylvania in 1911 and later studied in England, France, and Germany. Her first book, published in 1918, was *Reconstruction in Louisiana after 1868*. By the end of her career, she had written six books and served as the first woman president of the Southern Historical Association. For more, see Carol K. Bleser, "The Three Women Presidents of the Southern Historical Association: Ella Lonn, Kathryn Abby Hanna, and Mary Elizabeth Massey," *Southern Studies* 20 (Summer 1981): 101–10.

12. Ella Lonn, *Foreigners in the Union Army and Navy* (Baton Rouge: Louisiana State University Press, 1951), 648–49; Reinhart, ed. and trans., *Two Germans*, xxi, 178. Earl Hess, author of *A German in the Yankee Fatherland: The Civil War Letters of Henry A. Kircher* (Kent, Ohio: Kent State University Press, 1983), made this comment in an e-mail to Joseph R. Reinhart, September 10, 2002. See also Robertson Jr., *Soldiers Blue and Gray*, 27; and William C. Burton, *Melting Pot Soldiers: The Union's Ethnic Regiments* (New York: Fordham University Press, 1988).

13. Robertson Jr., *Soldiers Blue and Gray*, 27.

14. Bell Irvin Wiley, *The Life of Johnny Reb: The Common Soldier of the Confederacy* (1943; rpt., Baton Rouge: Louisiana State University Press, 1978), 323–24.

15. Jordan, "Germans," 143; diary entry dated April 25, 1863, in Arthur James Lyon Fremantle, *Three Months in the Southern States, April–June 1863* (1863; rpt., Lincoln: University of Nebraska Press, 1991), 53, 55; Olmsted, *A Journey through Texas*, 150. In 1860, San Antonio counted four thousand Mexicans, thirty-five hundred Americans, and three thousand Germans. Immigrants from German-speaking regions of Europe also constituted a large percentage of the inhabitants on the surrounding farms. Lonn, *Foreigners in the Confederacy*, 22.

16. Reinhart, ed. and trans., *Two Germans*, xxxi–xxxii; Robertson Jr., *Soldiers Blue and Gray*, 7.

17. The only predominantly German counties to approve secession were Austin, Comal, and Colorado, but they were not on the frontier. For more on what Texans did to contain the Indians, see David Paul Smith, *Frontier Defense in the Civil War: Texas' Rangers and Rebels* (College Station: Texas A&M University Press, 1992).

18. The vote was taken alphabetically and the first delegate to declare opposition was Houston's ally Thomas Hughes of Williamson County. Besides Hughes and James W. Throckmorton, the other six to vote against the ordinance

were W. H. Johnson, L. H. Williams, and George Wright from Lamar County; J. D. Rains and A. P. Shuford from Wood County; and Joshua Johnson from Titus County. Ralph A. Wooster, *Texas and Texans in the Civil War* (Austin: Eakin Press, 1995), 13. Voters approved the ordinance by a vote of 46,129 to 14,697 on February 23. The total number of votes was 60,950, down from the 63,423 counted in the 1860 presidential election. However, the number of Texans who voted for John C. Breckenridge (47,548) was almost exactly the same as the number who condoned secession (46,153). Wooster, *Texas and Texans*, 13. Texas had a rich cultural diversity that included not only Spanish, Mexican, and German towns but also French, Irish, English, Italians, Bohemians, Hungarians, Swedes, and Norwegians scattered in small settlements. While the number of Mexicans was certainly significant, they were not generally well regarded and not always politically active. Although Europeans could also be looked on with disfavor, that feeling did not usually involve the prejudices aimed at most Mexicans. There were some Mexican Americans who took part in the Civil War and served with distinction on the Confederate side, but the majority of Mexican descent remained passive and unaffected. For more on the various ethnic groups, see Lonn, *Foreigners in the Confederacy*, 13–23, 425. See also Walter L. Buenger, *Secession and the Union in Texas* (Austin: University of Texas Press, 1984); Walter L. Buenger, "Secession and the Texas German Community: Editor Lindheimer vs. Editor Flake," *Southwestern Historical Quarterly* 82 (April 1979): 379–402; Walter L. Buenger, "Unionism on the Texas Frontier, 1859–1861," *Arizona and the West* 22 (Autumn 1980): 237–54; Frank H. Smyrl, "Unionism in Texas, 1856–1861," *Southwestern Historical Quarterly* 68 (October 1964): 172–95; and Dale Baum, *The Shattering of Texas Unionism: Politics in the Lone Star State during the Civil War Era* (Baton Rouge: Louisiana State University Press, 1998).

19. "Regulations Respecting Alien Enemies" passed Congress on August 8, 1861. "A Proclamation by the President of the Confederate States," August 15, 1861, *A Compilation of the Messages and Papers of the Confederacy*, 2 vols. (Nashville: United States Publishing Co., 1905), 1:131–32.

20. Report of Hamilton P. Bee, October 21, 1862, U.S. War Department, *The War of the Rebellion: A Compilation of the Official Records of the Union and Confederate Armies*, 128 vols. (Washington, D.C.: 1880–1900), 1st ser., 53:454–55 (hereinafter cited as *O.R.*; all references are to the first series unless otherwise indicated).

21. Andrews, "German Pioneers in Texas," 38–39; Report of Hamilton P. Bee, October 21, 1862; Robert W. Shook, "The Battle of the Nueces, August 10, 1862," *Southwestern Historical Quarterly* 66 (July 1962): 32; Claude Elliott, "Union Sentiment in Texas, 1861–1865," *Southwestern Historical Quarterly* 50 (April 1947): 455. A German later said that at the beginning of the war there

had been a plan to take Austin and San Antonio and hold the cities until Union troops arrived. Some of the more radical wanted to capture weapons but were prevented by more sensible Germans.

22. Report of Hamilton P. Bee, October 21, 1862; O. M. Roberts, *Texas*, vol. 11 of *Confederate Military History*, ed. Clement A. Evans (Atlanta: Confederate Publishing Co., 1899), 68. Confederate troops included the Thirty-second Texas Cavalry. See also Carl L. Duaine, *The Dead Men Wore Boots: An Account of the 32nd Texas Volunteer Cavalry, C.S.A.* (Austin: San Felipe Press, 1966).

23. Martial Law Decree, June 14, 1862, *New Braunfelser Zeitung*; entry dated April 25, 1863, in Fremantle, *Three Months*, 54. The *New Braunfelser Zeitung*, one of the most influential of the German newspapers, had supported secession and was strongly pro-Southern. Based in Comal County, the German population around New Braunfels did not have to worry about Indians. Jordan, *German Seed in Texas Soil*, 183. See also Hermann Seele, *A Short Sketch of Comal County, Texas* (New Braunfels, Tex.: Zeitung, 1885).

24. R. H. Williams, *With the Border Ruffians: Memories of the Far West, 1852–1868* (New York: E. P. Dutton and Co., 1907), 236–37. For an examination of the war along the Mexican border, see James A. Irby, *Backdoor at Bagdad: The Civil War on the Rio Grande* (El Paso: Texas Western Press, 1977); and Robert W. Delaney, "Matamoras, Port for Texas during the Civil War," *Southwestern Historical Quarterly* 58 (April 1955): 473–87.

25. Williams, *With the Border Ruffians*, 232.

26. Andrews, "German Pioneers in Texas," 36; *San Antonio Herald*, July 19, 1862; *Dallas Herald*, June 14, 1862; entry dated August 5, 1862, in "Diary of Desmond Pulaski Hopkins," supplied by G. A. McNaughton to the *San Antonio Express*, January 13, 1918, typescript, Center for American History, University of Texas, Austin.

27. Rudolf Coreth to family, August 26, 1862, in *Lone Star and Double Eagle: Civil War Letters of a German-Texas Family*, ed. Minetta Altgelt Goyne (Fort Worth: Texas Christian University Press, 1982), 66; Report of C. D. McRae, August 18, 1862, *O.R.*, 9:615; entry dated August 22, 1862, in August Hoffman, "Memoir of August Hoffman," typescript, Center for American History, University of Texas, Austin.

28. The estimate of Germans wounded or killed in the battle vary. Following the fight the Confederates were interred in a common grave, but the Germans were left unburied, and their remains were not recovered until August 1865 when they were reinterred in Comfort, Texas. The monument read, *Treuer der Union*. Shook, "The Battle of the Nueces," 39–41. See also John W. Sansom, *Battle of the Nueces in Kinney County, Texas, Aug. 10th, 1862* (San Antonio: n.p., 1905); Andrews, "German Pioneers in Texas," 40; and Lonn, *Foreigners in the*

Confederacy, 423–36. For a revisionist version, see Richard Selcer and William Paul Burrier, "What Really Happened on the Nueces River: James Duff, a Good Soldier or 'The Butcher of Fredericksburg?'" *North and South: The Magazine of Civil War Conflict*, January 1998, 56–61. See also Williams, *With the Border Ruffians*, 250; entry dated August 27, 1862, in Thomas C. Smith, *Here's Yer Mule: The Diary of Thomas C. Smith, 3rd Sergeant, Company 'G,' Wood's Regiment, 32nd Texas Cavalry, C.S.A.: March 30, 1862–December 31, 1862* (Waco: Little Texan Press, 1958), 19; and entry dated August 22, 1862, in Hoffman, "Memoir of August Hoffman."

29. Entry dated August 27, 1862, in Thomas C. Smith, *Here's Yer Mule*, 19.

30. E. P. Turner to J. P. Flewellen, December 6, 1862, *O.R.*, 15:890. Flewellen served as superintendent of conscripts at Austin.

31. Special Orders, no. 35, January 5, 1863, *O.R.*, 15:931; J. Bankhead Magruder to F. R. Lubbock, February 11, 1862, *O.R.*, 15:974–75. See also Martin M. Kenney, *An Historical and Descriptive Sketch of Austin County, Texas* (Brenham, Tex.: Banner Print, 1876); W. A. Trenckmann, *Austin County: Beilage zum Bellville Wochenblatt* (Bellville, Tex.: Wochenblatt, 1899); Frank Lotto, *Fayette County: Her History and Her People* (Schulenburg, Tex.: n.p., 1902); A. J. Rosenthal, "Fayette County," in *Schütze's Jahrbuch für Texas* (Austin: A. Schütze, 1883); and Leonie R. Weyand and Houston Wade, *An Early History of Fayette County* (La Grange, Tex.: LaGrange Journal, 1936).

32. Charles A. Leuschner, *The Diary of Charles A. Leuschner*, ed. Charles D. Spurlin (Austin: Eakin Press, 1992), vi; diary entries dated March 28, 1864, and March 4, 1865, in Julius Giesecke, *Giesecke's Civil War Diary: The Story of Company G of the Fourth Regiment of the First Texas Cavalry Brigade of the Army of the Confederate States of America (1861–1865)*, trans. Charles Patrick (Manor, Tex.: Patrick Historical Research, 1999), 54, 64.

33. Olmsted, *A Journey through Texas*, 181; Robert B. Shook, "German Unionism in Texas during the Civil War and Reconstruction" (PhD diss., North Texas State College, 1957), 16, 20. In the 1860 presidential election, New Braunfels voters had given John C. Breckinridge 137 votes; John Bell, 15; and Abraham Lincoln, 0. A comparison of Comal and surroundings counties can be found in Judith Dykes-Hoffman, "'Treue Der Union': German Texas Women on the Civil War Homefront" (PhD diss., Southwest Texas State University, 1996), 22, 28, 78. See also Buenger, *Secession and the Union in Texas*.

34. Many Germans committed to the Confederate cause and joined the Rebel army. See Gregg Woodall, "German Confederates from Comal County: Some German Immigrants Made the Difficult Decision to Embrace the Confederacy," *Columbiad: A Quarterly Review of the War between the States* 2 (Winter 1999): 46–56. See also E. P. Petty to "Dear Wife," December 5, 1861, in *Journey to Pleasant*

Hill: The Civil War Letters of Captain Elijah P. Petty, Walker's Texas Division CSA, ed. Norman D. Brown (San Antonio: Institute of Texan Cultures, 1982), 12. Petty called Germans the "Dutch," or *Deutsch*, meaning German. For more, see Dykes-Hoffman, "*Treue Der Union*," 74–75. Although Rudolf joined in New Braunfels, not all men of military age enlisted. On April 20, 1861, T. J. Thomas reported that local residents generally avoided enrolling officers, and he believed nothing short of a draft would force them to enlist. Lonn, *Foreigners in the Confederacy*, 312. The quote is found in Rudolf Coreth to family, November 13, 1861, in Goyne, *Lone Star and Double Eagle*, 23.

35. Rudolf Coreth to family, November 3, 1861, and February 9 [8], 1862, in Goyne, *Lone Star and Double Eagle*, 19, 41.

36. Three Coreth brothers were of military age. Carl Coreth was born January 16, 1837; Rudolf Coreth was born May 7, 1838; and Johann was born February 19, 1845. Young Joseph was eight years old. For the quote, see Rudolf Coreth to Carl Coreth, [April 4, 1862?], in Goyne, *Lone Star and Double Eagle*, 50.

37. Carl had returned home to be with his wife, Hedwig, for the birth of their first child. Rudolf Coreth to father, [June 1863], and Ernst Coreth to Rudolf, [September 20, 1863?], in Goyne, *Lone Star and Double Eagle*, 87, 105; Duaine, *The Dead Men Wore Boots*, 98.

38. Rudolf Coreth to family, December 23, 1864, and January 12, 1865, in Goyne, *Lone Star and Double Eagle*, 154–55, 157. Carl Coreth died on January 13, 1865, and was buried in an unmarked grave at San Augustine, Texas. His son, Karl Coreth Jr., had been born on December 3, 1864. Carl Coreth to parents, January 12, 1865, in Goyne, *Lone Star and Double Eagle*, 157.

39. Ernst Coreth to Rudolf Coreth, May 19, 1865, and Rudolf Coreth to family, May 19, 1865, in Goyne, *Lone Star and Double Eagle*, 173–74. Because of European laws, Rudolf Coreth did not remain buried in the original plot. His family did not realize that a periodic fee was required to retain claim to a burial site, and at some point his body was moved. Therefore all three Coreth brothers who fought for the Confederacy lie in unmarked graves. Goyne, *Lone Star and Double Eagle*, 174, 202.

40. Jordan, "Germans." See also Charles William Ramsdell, *Reconstruction in Texas* (New York: Columbia University Press, 1910).

TWO. THE WAR WITHIN

1. Laurence M. Hauptman, *Between Two Fires: American Indians in the Civil War* (New York: Free Press, 1995), 12.

2. Some four thousand people in the Cherokee nation were slaves. Emmett

Starr, *History of the Cherokee Indians and Their Legends and Folklore* (Oklahoma City: Warden Co., 1921), 261; W. Craig Gaines, *The Confederate Cherokees: John Drew's Regiment of Mounted Rifles* (Baton Rouge: Louisiana State University Press, 1989), 1. See also LeRoy H. Fischer, *The Civil War Era in Indian Territory* (Los Angeles: Lorrin L. Morrison, 1974); Theda Perdue and Michael D. Green, introduction to *The American Indian in the Civil War, 1862–1865*, by Annie Heloise Abel (1919; rpt., Lincoln: University of Nebraska Press, 1992); James I. Robertson Jr., *Soldiers Blue and Gray* (Columbia: University of South Carolina Press, 1988), 29; and Bell Irvin Wiley, *The Life of Johnny Reb: The Common Soldier of the Confederacy* (1943; rpt., Baton Rouge: Louisiana State University Press, 1978), 325. Other useful books include George Brown Tindall, *Natives and Newcomers: Ethnic Southerners and Southern Ethnics* (Athens: University of Georgia Press, 1995); Wiley Britton, *The Civil War on the Border*, 2 vols. (New York: G. P. Putnam's Sons, 1904); Wiley Britton, *The Union Indian Brigade in the Civil War* (Kansas City: Franklin Hudson, 1922); Jay Monaghan, *Civil War on the Western Border, 1854–1865* (Boston: Little, Brown, and Co., 1955); W. W. Newcomb Jr., *The Indians of Texas: From Prehistory to Modern* (Austin: University of Texas Press, 1961); Theda Perdue, *Slavery and the Evolution of Cherokee Society, 1540–1866* (Knoxville: University of Tennessee Press, 1979); Robert M. Utley, *The Indian Frontier of the American West, 1846–1890* (Albuquerque: University of New Mexico Press, 1984); Carolyn Ross Johnston, *Cherokee Women in Crisis: Trail of Tears, Civil War, and Allotment, 1838–1907* (Tuscaloosa: University of Alabama Press, 2003); Andrew K. Frank, *Creeks and Southerners: Biculturalism on the Early American Frontier* (Lincoln: University of Nebraska Press, 2005).

3. William M. (Buck) Walton, *An Epitome of My Life: Civil War Reminiscences* (Austin: Waterloo Press, 1965), 77–78.

4. Herbert Gambrell, "Mirabeau Buonaparte Lamar," in *The New Handbook of Texas*, ed. Ron Tyler, 6 vols. (Austin: Texas State Historical Association, 1996), 4:37–39; Stanley E. Siegel, *The Poet President of Texas: The Life of Mirabeau B. Lamar, President of the Republic of Texas* (Austin: Jenkins, 1977); Robert A. Calvert and Arnoldo De León, *The History of Texas* (Arlington Heights, Ill.: Harlan Davidson, 1990), 85–86.

5. See Anne J. Bailey, *Between the Enemy and Texas: Parsons's Texas Cavalry in the Civil War* (Fort Worth: Texas Christian University Press, 1989), 233–34; Compiled Service Records of Confederate Soldiers Who Served in Organizations from the State of Texas, Morgan's Battalion, National Archives and Records Administration, Washington, D.C.; Kenneth F. Neighbours, *Indian Exodus: Texas Indian Affairs, 1835–1859* (San Antonio: Nortex, 1973); Utley, *Indian Frontier*; W. E. S. Dickerson, "Indian Relation," in Tyler, *The New Handbook of Texas*, 3:832–36; and Hauptman, *Between Two Fires*, 3.

6. Alvin M. Josephy Jr., *The Civil War in the American West* (New York: Alfred A. Knopf, 1991), 284–87.

7. Ibid., 105–12, 137–38; Wallace J. Schutz and Walter N. Trenerry, *Abandoned by Lincoln: A Military Biography of General John Pope* (Urbana: University of Illinois Press, 1990), 175–78.

8. Annie H. Abel, "The Indians in the Civil War," *American Historical Review* 15 (January 1910): 281–96; Edward E. Dale, "The Cherokees in the Confederacy," *Journal of Southern History* 13 (May 1947): 159–85; Lary C. Rampp and Donald L. Rampp, *The Civil War in the Indian Territory* (Austin: Presidial Press, 1975).

9. About North Georgia, "John Ross: A North Georgia Notable," http://ngeorgia.com/people/ross.html (accessed April 21, 2005).

10. Perdue and Green, introduction to Abel, *American Indian*, 1–11. See also Theda Perdue, "Indians in Southern History," in *Indians in American History*, ed. Frederick E. Hoxie (Arlington Heights, Ill.: Forum Press, 1988), 137–57; Perdue, *Slavery*; Daniel F. Littlefield Jr., *Africans and Creeks: From the Colonial Period to the Civil War* (Westport, Conn.: Greenwood Press, 1979); William G. McLoughlin, *The Cherokee Ghost Dance: Essays on the Southeastern Indians, 1789–1861* (Macon, Ga.: Mercer University Press, 1984); Daniel F. Littlefield Jr., *Africans and Seminoles: From Removal to Emancipation* (Westport, Conn.: Greenwood Press, 1977); Wilson Lumpkin, *The Removal of the Cherokee Indians from Georgia* (New York: Dodd Mead and Co., 1907); Ronald N. Satz, *American Indian Policy in the Jacksonian Era* (Lincoln: University of Nebraska Press, 1975); Michael D. Green, *The Politics of Indian Removal: Creek Government and Society in Crisis* (Lincoln: University of Nebraska Press, 1981); and Martha Condray Searcy, "The Introduction of African Slavery into the Creek Indian Nation," *Georgia Historical Quarterly* 66 (Spring 1982): 21–32.

11. Perdue and Green, introduction to Abel, *American Indian*, 3.

12. S. B. Maxey to S. S. Anderson, February 7, 1864, U.S. War Department, *The War of the Rebellion: A Compilation of the Official Records of the Union and Confederate Armies*, 128 vols. (Washington, D.C.: 1880–1900), 1st ser., 53:963–66 (hereinafter cited as *O.R.*; all references are to the first series unless otherwise indicated). See also John C. Waugh, *Samuel Bell Maxey and the Confederate Indians* (Abilene, Tex.: McWhiney Foundation Press, 1995); and Nancy Hobson, "Samuel Bell Maxey as Confederate Commander of Indian Territory," *Journal of the West* 12 (1973): 424–38.

13. Frank Cunningham, *General Stand Watie's Confederate Indians* (1959; rpt., Norman: University of Oklahoma Press, 1998), 1–14.

14. See Kenny A. Franks, *Stand Watie and the Agony of the Cherokee Nation* (Memphis: Memphis State University Press, 1979); Wilfred Knight, *Red Fox: Stand Watie's Civil War Years in Indian Territory* (Glendale, Calif.: A. H. Clark

Co., 1988); Gaines, *The Confederate Cherokees*; and Kenny A. Franks, "Stand Watie," in *Encyclopedia of the Confederacy*, ed. Richard N. Current, 4 vols. (New York: Simon and Schuster, 1993), 4:1692–94. See also Cunningham, *General Stand Watie's Confederate Indians*. Those Cherokees who escaped capture in Georgia became known as the Eastern Cherokees. Moreover, Allen Ross, one of the chief's sons, was involved in the assassination plot, although no one was ever prosecuted by either the Cherokee tribe or the U.S. government. See also Hauptman, *Between Two Fires*, 44; and Thurman Wilkins, *Cherokee Tragedy: The Ridge Family and the Decimation of a People* (New York: Macmillan, 1970).

15. Gaines, *The Confederate Cherokees*, 8. See also Thomas W. Cutrer, *Ben McCulloch and the Frontier Military Tradition* (Chapel Hill: University of North Carolina Press, 1993). William Seward is quoted in Annie Heloise Abel, *The American Indian as Slaveholder and Secessionist* (1915; rpt., Lincoln: University of Nebraska Press, 1992), 58–59; George E. Baker, ed., *The Works of William H. Seward*, 5 vols. (Boston: Houghton Mifflin and Co., 1853–84), 4:363.

16. Gaines, *The Confederate Cherokees*, 8.

17. See Frederick W. Allsopp, *Albert Pike: A Biography* (Little Rock: Parker-Harper, 1928); Robert Lipscomb Duncan, *Reluctant General: The Life and Times of Albert Pike* (New York: E. P. Dutton, 1961); Anne J. Bailey, "Albert Pike," in Current, *Encyclopedia of the Confederacy*, 3:1210–11; and Gaines, *The Confederate Cherokees*, 4.

18. John Ross to Ben McCulloch, August 24, 1861, *O.R.*, 3:673–76.

19. Ibid. An enclosure included with Ross's letter detailed the proceedings and the resolutions that were passed.

20. Mary Jane Warde, *George Washington Grayson and the Creek Nation, 1843–1920* (Norman: University of Oklahoma Press, 1999), 58; Angie Debo, *The Road to Disappearance: A History of the Creek Indians* (Norman: University of Oklahoma Press, 1941), 144–45; Arrell Morgan Gibson, *The American Indian: Prehistory to the Present* (Norman: University of Oklahoma Press, 1980), 367–68; Duane Champagne, *Social Order and Political Change: Constitutional Government among the Cherokee, the Choctaw, the Chickasaws, and the Creek* (Stanford, Calif.: Stanford University Press, 1992), 203; William G. McLoughlin, *After the Trail of Tears: The Cherokees' Struggle for Sovereignty, 1839–1880* (Chapel Hill: University of North Carolina Press, 1992), 120, 156–57; Christine Schultz White and Benton R. White, *Now the Wolf has Come: The Creek Nation in the Civil War* (College Station: Texas A&M University Press, 1996), 23. See also Perdue and Green, introduction to Abel, *American Indian*, 1–5.

21. See Lela J. McBride, *Opothleyaholo and the Loyal Muskogee: Their Flight to Kansas in the Civil War* (Jefferson, N.C.: McFarland and Co., 2000); and Carter Blue Clark, "Opothleyohola and the Creeks during the Civil War," in

Indian Leaders: Oklahoma's First Statesmen, ed. H. Glen Jordan and Thomas M. Holm (Oklahoma City: Oklahoma Historical Society, 1979), 49–63. See also Britton, *Union Indian Brigade*. The pro-Union leader and elderly Upper Creek was known variously as Opothleyaholo, Hopoeithleyohola, Hopothleyahola, and Opothle Yahola. The Upper Creeks came from the upper tributaries of the Chattahoochee River in Alabama and Georgia; the Lower Creeks came from towns further down the river. The First Creek Regiment of the Confederacy was composed of Lower Creeks and was led by Colonel Daniel McIntosh (a Baptist minister) and his brother Lieutenant Colonel Chilly McIntosh.

22. Cunningham, *General Stand Watie's Confederate Indians*, 28.

23. Ibid. See also Brad Agnew, foreword to Cunningham, *General Stand Watie's Confederate Indians*, vii–x. Only a small number of Cherokee participated in the Battle of Wilson's Creek. See William Garrett Piston and Richard W. Hatcher III, *Wilson's Creek: The Second Battle of the Civil War and the Men Who Fought It* (Chapel Hill: University of North Carolina Press, 2000), 92.

24. Gaines, *The Confederate Cherokees*, 11–19.

25. Ibid., 20–23.

26. See Cunningham, *General Stand Watie's Confederate Indians*.

27. S. R. Curtis to Earl Van Dorn, March 9, 1862, *O.R.*, 8:194; Curtis to J. C. Kelton, March 13, 1862, *O.R.*, 8:195.

28. Quoted in William L. Shea and Earl J. Hess, *Pea Ridge: Civil War Campaign in the West* (Chapel Hill: University of North Carolina Press, 1992), 320. A highly critical account of the actions of the Native Americans is found in John W. Noble, "Battle of Pea Ridge, or Elk Horn Tavern," in Military Order of the Loyal Legion of the United States, *War Papers and Personal Reminiscences, 1861–1865* (St. Louis: Becktold, 1892), 211–42. Noble claimed that an occasional "ward of the nation" could be seen "with the harness of an artillery horse on, the trace chains clanging at his heels and a collar over his neck, exclaiming as such ha[d] been known to do on other occasions, 'Me big In'gen, big as horse'" (228). Other studies of the battle include Walter L. Brown, "Pea Ridge: Gettysburg of the West," *Arkansas Historical Quarterly* 15 (Spring 1956): 3–16; Albert Castel, "A New View of the Battle of Pea Ridge," *Missouri Historical Review* 62 (January 1968): 136–51; Edwin C. Bearss, "The First Day at Pea Ridge, March 7, 1862," *Arkansas Historical Quarterly* 17 (Summer 1958): 132–54.

29. Dabney H. Maury to Curtis, March 14, 1862, *O.R.*, 8:195; Maury, the assistant adjutant general, was writing for Van Dorn. On April 3, the First Confederate Congress, during its first session, appropriated $389,725.42 to carry into effect treaty stipulations made with the Indians and "to meet current and contingent expenses of the superintendency of Indian Affairs and the different agencies" until November 30, 1862.

30. Shea and Hess, *Pea Ridge*, 320. Drew's regiment dissolved after Pea Ridge, with many Indians defecting to the Union side. See Gaines, *The Confederate Cherokees*, for more on Drew's regiment.

31. Hauptman, *Between Two Fires*, 41–61.

32. S. S. Scott to James A. Seddon, *O.R.*, 4th ser., 2:352–56.

33. One of Cynthia Ann Parker's two sons with Comanche chief Pete Nocona was Quanah Parker. Eventually a Comanche chief himself, Quanah fought the U.S. Army before moving his people to a reservation in the Indian Territory. He became one of the most important Comanche leaders of the late nineteenth century. For the story of Cynthia Ann's life, see Margaret S. Hacker, *Cynthia Ann Parker: The Life and the Legend* (El Paso: Texas Western Press, 1990); Grace Jackson, *Cynthia Ann Parker* (San Antonio: Naylor, 1959); and James T. DeShields, *Cynthia Ann Parker: The Story of Her Capture* (1886; rpt., Dallas: Chama Press, 1991).

34. "More Murders in Parker County," in J. W. Wilbarger, *Indian Depredations in Texas* (Austin: Hutchings Printing House, 1889), 521–22.

35. T. T. Ewell, *Hood County History* (1895), reprinted in *Hood County History in Picture and Story* (Fort Worth: Historical Publishers, 1970), 76–77. For more on the Indian problems in Confederate Texas, see David Paul Smith, *Frontier Defense in the Civil War: Texas' Rangers and Rebels* (College Station: Texas A&M University Press, 1992); for the Choctaw and Chickasaw soldiers, see 64, 85. DeMorse is quoted in Waugh, *Sam Bell Maxey*, 47.

36. Mary Jane Warde, "Refugees, Civil War," in *The Encyclopedia of Oklahoma History and Culture*, Oklahoma Historical Society, www.ok-history.mus.ok.us/enc/rfgscw.htm (accessed June 14, 2005).

37. Ibid.

38. Stand Watie to the governors of the Choctaws and Chickasaw Nations, August 9, 1863, *O.R.*, vol. 22, pt. 2, 961–62.

39. For more, see Clyde A. Milner II, Carol A. O'Connor, and Martha A. Sandweiss, eds., *The Oxford History of the American West* (New York: Oxford University Press, 1994), 179; Josephy, *Civil War*, 306–12.

40. Agnew, foreword to Cunningham, *General Stand Watie's Confederate Indians*, vii–x. See also Waugh, *Samuel Bell Maxey*.

41. Hauptman, *Between Two Fires*, 42; Warde, "Refugees, Civil War"; Warde, *George Washington Grayson*, 84.

42. Warde, *George Washington Grayson*, 83.

43. William T. Hagan, *Taking Indian Lands: The Cherokee (Jerome) Commission, 1889–1893* (Norman: University of Oklahoma Press, 2003), 7–8; Warde, *George Washington Grayson*, 84.

1. William C. Davis, *"A Government of Our Own": The Making of the Confederacy* (New York: Free Press, 1994), 290, 332–33; *Atlanta Southern Confederacy*, April 11, 1861; *Montgomery Weekly Advertiser*, April 24, 1862; *Nashville Union and American*, April 26, 1861; *Weekly Montgomery Confederation*, May 3, 1861. Louisiana governor Thomas D. Moore accepted some 1,500 Native Guards as part of the state's militia on May 2, 1861, and gave commissions to black officers. Unlike in other Southern states, in prewar Louisiana, the presence of black soldiers in the militia was not unusual. For more, see James G. Hollandsworth Jr., *The Louisiana Native Guards: The Black Military Experience in the Civil War* (Baton Rouge: Louisiana State University Press, 1995); Charles H. Wesley, "The Employment of Negroes as Soldiers in the Confederate Army," *Journal of Negro History* 4 (July 1919): 239–53; Dudley Taylor Cornish, *The Sable Arm: Negro Troops in the Union Army, 1861–1865* (1956; rpt., Lawrence: University Press of Kansas, 1987); and William A. Gladstone, *United States Colored Troops, 1863–1867* (Gettysburg, Pa.: Thomas Publications, 1990).

2. One of the best recent overviews of the role of African Americans in the U.S. military appears in Noah Andrew Trudeau, *Like Men of War: Black Troops in the Civil War, 1862–1865* (New York: Little, Brown, and Co., 1998), 9–10. Moreover, in the last decade the number of books on blacks in Union blue has increased significantly. Unlike other fields in Civil War history, this is not one that has been exhausted by researchers; much is still to be learned.

3. *New Orleans Daily Crescent*, May 29, 1861. See also Hollandsworth Jr., *The Louisiana Native Guards*; and Lawrence Lee Hewitt, "An Ironic Route to Glory: Louisiana's Native Guards at Port Hudson," in *Black Soldiers in Blue: African American Troops in the Civil War Era*, ed. John David Smith (Chapel Hill: University of North Carolina Press, 2002), 78–106.

4. The First Regiment of the Native Guards, on September 27, 1862, became the first black regiment to receive recognition by the federal government. Although other black regiments had appeared by this time, including Senator James Lane's First Regiment of Kansas Colored Volunteers, the Native Guards were the first to earn official status. See Hollandsworth Jr., *The Louisiana Native Guards*, and Hewitt, "An Ironic Route to Glory," for more on the battle of Port Hudson. For an early look at the units raised in Kansas, see Dudley Taylor Cornish, "Kansas Negro Regiments in the Civil War," *Kansas Historical Quarterly* 20 (1952–53): 417–29. Writing just a few years after the end of World War II and the integration of the U.S. Army, Cornish pointed out that only three book-length studies about black soldiers had been published since the end of the Civil War; at that time the most recent had been in 1891. Cornish, who became

an authority on black soldiers, had written his dissertation at the University of Colorado, Boulder, on the subject in 1949.

5. Craig L. Symonds, *Stonewall Jackson of the West: Patrick Cleburne and the Civil War* (Lawrence: University Press of Kansas, 1997), 182–92.

6. Ibid., 188–89. This proposal, made by a Confederate, has been the subject of much discussion in recent years.

7. Symonds, *Stonewall Jackson of the West*, 194; William H. T. Walker to Jefferson Davis, January 12, 1864, and Jefferson Davis to William H. T. Walker, January 13, 1864, U.S. War Department, *The War of the Rebellion: A Compilation of the Official Records of the Union and Confederate Armies*, 128 vols. (Washington, D.C.: 1880–1900), 1st ser., vol. 52, pt. 2, 595–97 (hereinafter cited as *O.R.*; all references are to the first series unless otherwise indicated). President Davis told Walker: "Deeming it to be injurious to the public service that such a subject should be mooted, or even known to be entertained by persons possessed of the confidence and respect of the people, I have concluded that the best policy under the circumstances will be to avoid all publicity, and the Secretary of War has therefore written to General Johnston requesting him to convey to those concerned my desire that it should be kept private. If it be kept out of the public journals its ill effect will be much lessened." See also Russell K. Brown, *To the Manner Born: The Life of General William H. T. Walker* (Athens: University of Georgia Press, 1994), 201.

8. *Richmond Daily Examiner*, November 8, 1864; Mark M. Hull, "Concerning the Emancipation of the Slaves" in *A Meteor Shining Brightly: Essays on Maj. Gen. Patrick R. Cleburne*, ed. Mauriel Phillips Joslyn (Milledgeville, Ga.: Terrell House Publishing, 1997), 143–69. A copy of the proposal is found on pages 170–77.

9. Surrender demand of John Bell Hood, October 13, 1864, *O.R.*, vol. 39, pt. 1, 718; entry dated October 12, 1864, Charles Dennison Brandon Diary, Misc.—Brandon, Charles Dennison, Kansas State Historical Society, Topeka.

10. L. Johnson to R. D. Mussey, October 17, 1864, *O.R.*, vol. 39, pt. 1, 719–20; William E. Bevens, *Reminiscences of a Private: William E. Bevens of the First Arkansas Infantry, C.S.A.*, ed. Daniel E. Sutherland (Fayetteville: University of Arkansas Press, 1992), 199.

11. Trudeau, *Like Men of War*, 279.

12. *Charleston Mercury*, October 24, 1864; Philip Daingerfield Stephenson, *The Civil War Memoir of Philip Daingerfield Stephenson, D.D.*, ed. Nathaniel Cheairs Hughes Jr. (Conway: University of Central Arkansas Press, 1995), 255; Bevens, *Reminiscences of a Private*, 199.

13. Johnson to Mussey, October 17, 1864; *Charleston Mercury*, November 7, 1864, reprinted from the *Cincinnati Commercial*, October 26, 1864.

14. Trudeau, *Like Men of War*, 279; George Wm. Brent to J. B. Hood,

November 12, 1864, *O.R.*, vol. 39, pt. 3, 914; *Charleston Mercury*, October 24, 1864; Lee Kennett, *Marching through Georgia: The Story of Soldiers and Civilians during Sherman's Campaign* (New York: Harper Collins, 1995), 220.

15. Howell Cobb to James A. Seddon, January 8, 1865, *O.R.*, 4th ser., 3:1009–10.

16. The issue of blacks in the South is discussed in William C. Davis, *Look Away! A History of the Confederate States of America* (New York: Free Press, 2002), 157.

17. Northern states contributed 19 percent of the total. African Americans made up 9 to 10 percent of the Union army; sixteen blacks received the Medal of Honor. John David Smith, "Let Us All Be Grateful That We Have Colored Troops That Will Fight," in Smith, *Black Soldiers in Blue*, 1.

18. Smith, "Let Us All Be Grateful," 23.

19. Ibid., 17–18.

20. Michael T. Meier, "Lorenzo Thomas and the Recruitment of Blacks in the Mississippi Valley, 1863–1865," in Smith, *Black Soldiers in Blue*, 249–75; Smith, "Let Us All Be Grateful," 25.

21. Smith, "Let Us All Be Grateful," 44–45. See also Hewitt, "An Ironic Route to Glory"; and Richard Lowe, "Battle on the Levee: The Fight at Milliken's Bend," in Smith, *Black Soldiers in Blue*, 78–106. For the events following Mound Plantation, see Anne J. Bailey, "A Texas Cavalry Raid: Reaction to Black Soldiers and Contrabands," in *Black Flag over Dixie: Racial Atrocities and Reprisals in the Civil War*, ed. Gregory J. W. Urwin (Carbondale: Southern Illinois University Press, 2004), 19–33.

22. Pension files of Matthew Jarman, Company E, Forty-sixth USCT, National Archives and Records Administration, Washington, D.C. (hereinafter cited as NARA). Cook, who was in the same company as Jarman, was testifying on behalf of Jarman's widow. Cook attributed the death of Jarman to "fatigue" elicited by a forced march following the battle, although many of the black soldiers "believed he was killed by being struck on the head by a rebel guard with butt of his gun because he could not keep up." Deposition of Wilson Chambers, pension files of Matthew Jarman. Edward Terry, whose name in 1905 was Edward Bell, suffered the fate of many black soldiers. Because the U.S. Army would not recognize their capture, they were denied pensions in the years following the war. See pension file of Alexander Grape, Company E, Forty-sixth USCT, NARA. Ironically, although he had been turned down, Terry was giving a deposition for one Alexander Grape, whom he did not recall. Charles Bogan was testifying on behalf of the widow of his nephew James Albert [Bogan]. See pension file of James Albert, Company G, Forty-sixth USCT, NARA. It was not uncommon for ex-slaves to drop their former owner's name after freedom or to change their last name completely.

23. Pension files of Samuel Anderson, Company E, Forty-sixth USCT, NARA. Slaves did not celebrate official emancipation in Texas until June 19, 1865. Anderson likely did not have the means to leave—such was the case with many former slaves who were forced to remain on farms and plantations because they had nowhere else to go. See also George W. Ingram to Martha F. Ingram, February 6, 1864, in *Civil War Letters of George W. and Martha F. Ingram, 1861–1865*, compiled by Henry L. Ingram (College Station: Texas A&M University, 1973), 68–69; and Bell Irvin Wiley, *The Life of Johnny Reb: The Common Soldier of the Confederacy* (1943; rpt., Baton Rouge: Louisiana State University Press, 1978), 314.

24. Special Orders, nos. 2 and 3, August 16, 1863, in *In the Saddle with the Texans: Day-by-Day with Parsons's Cavalry Brigade, 1862–1865*, ed. Anne J. Bailey (Abilene, Tex.: McWhiney Foundation Press, 2004), 217. This is the edited version of the brigade's original order book.

25. Smith, "Let Us All Be Grateful," 47. See also John Cimprich, "The Fort Pillow Massacre: Assessing the Evidence," in Smith, *Black Soldiers in Blue*, 150–68. For more on the treatment of black prisoners, see three chapters in Urwin, *Black Flag over Dixie*, 89–152: Albert Castel, "The Fort Pillow Massacre: An Examination of the Evidence"; Derek W. Frisby, "'Remember Fort Pillow!' Politics, Atrocity Propaganda, and the Evolution of Hard War"; and Gregory J. W. Urwin, "'We *Cannot* Treat . . . as Prisoners of War': Racial Atrocities and Reprisals in Civil War Arkansas."

26. W. T. Sherman to John A. Spooner, July 30, 1864, in *Sherman's Civil War: Selected Correspondence of William T. Sherman, 1860–1865*, ed. Brooks D. Simpson and Jean V. Berlin (Chapel Hill: University of North Carolina Press, 1999), 677–78; Cyrus Bussey to Samuel R. Curtis, January 13, 1863, quoted in "The Negro in the Military Service of the United States," Record Group 94, Adjutant General's Office, NARA; Samuel R. Curtis to Benjamin Prentiss, March 9, 1863, in "The Negro in the Military Service of the United States."

27. War Department General Orders No. 143, May 22, 1863, and Ulysses S. Grant to Henry Halleck, April 19, 1863, both in "The Negro in the Military Service of the United States"; Michael T. Meier, "Lorenzo Thomas," 250; Ira Berlin, Joseph P. Reidy, and Leslie S. Rowland, eds., *The Black Military Experience* (Cambridge: Cambridge University Press, 1982), 1–45. See also Benjamin Quarles, *The Negro in the Civil War* (1953; rpt., New York: DaCapo Press, 1989).

28. Lorenzo Thomas to Edwin Stanton, September 20, 1864, *O.R.*, 3rd ser., 4:733–34.

29. William T. Sherman to Thomas, June 21, 26, 1864, *O.R.*, vol. 39, pt. 2, 132; and 3rd ser., 4:434.

30. Stanton to Thomas, September 19, 1864, *O.R.*, 3rd ser., 4:733–34; Michael Fellman, "Lincoln and Sherman," in *Lincoln's Generals*, ed. Gabor S. Boritt (New

York: Oxford University Press, 1994), 127; William T. Sherman to Ellen Sherman, January 15, 1865, in Simpson and Berlin, *Sherman's Civil War*, 798.

31. W. T. Sherman to Thomas, June 21, 1864, *O.R.*, vol. 39, pt. 2, 132; W. T. Sherman to Spooner, July 30, 1864, enclosed in Mussey to Major [Charles W. Foster?], August 2, 1864, M-583 1864, Letters Received, ser. 360, Colored Troops Division, Record Group 94, Adjutant General's Office, NARA, quoted in Berlin, Reidy, and Rowland, *The Black Military Experience*, 110–11, and in Simpson and Berlin, *Sherman's Civil War*, 677–78. See also William C. Davis, *Look Away!*, 149; and *Houston Weekly Telegraph*, September 3, 1863.

32. George Mason Graham to P. G. T. Beauregard, January 26, 1866, George Mason Graham MSS, Virginia Historical Society, Richmond; William T. Sherman to Tom Ewing Jr., February 17, 1860, Thomas E. Ewing MSS, Library of Congress, Washington, D.C.; William T. Sherman to Hugh B. Ewing, August 13, 1859, William T. Sherman MSS, Ohio Historical Society, Columbus.

33. William T. Sherman to Ellen Sherman, April 17, 1863, and William T. Sherman to John Sherman, April 26, 1863, in Simpson and Berlin, *Sherman's Civil War*, 451–54, 459–63. See also Fellman, "Lincoln and Sherman," 141–42.

34. Special Field Order No. 16, June 3, 1864, *O.R.*, 3rd ser., 4:434.

35. William T. Sherman to Thomas, June 21, 1864, *O.R.*, vol. 39, pt. 2, 132; W. T. Sherman to Spooner, July 30, 1864. In spite of Sherman's evaluation of Georgia, at least 3,486 African American Georgians and more than 2,300 white Georgians joined the Union army. For more on this, see Robert S. Davis Jr., "White and Black in Blue: The Recruitment of Federal Units in Civil War North Georgia," *Georgia Historical Quarterly* 85 (Fall 2001), 355–56.

36. Stearns had also been one of the "Secret Six," a group of abolitionists who had financed John Brown's plans to liberate the slaves in Virginia in 1859. Mussey later reported that Stearns "found that the raising of colored troops was, if not opposed, regarded with distrust and suspicion by influential loyal Tennesseans, and some time elapsed before harmonious relations were established between Major Stearns and these gentlemen." Mussey to Foster, October 10, 1864, *O.R.*, 3rd ser., 4:763–74; *Nashville Daily Press*, October 3, 1863; Special Field Order No. 243, September 8, 1863, *O.R.*, 3rd ser., 3:786–87; Special Orders, no. 15, February 9, 1864, *O.R.*, 3rd ser., 4:90; Cornish, *The Sable Arm*, 235–38, 248–49.

37. Tennessee would eventually furnish around twenty thousand black soldiers. Under Lincoln's directive, "Slaves of loyal citizens [could] be enlisted into the service of the United States with their master's consent." The governor finally agreed to allow other blacks to enlist without their owner's permission if the government would give a voucher to the owner promising compensation upon arrival of a slave's emancipation papers (not to exceed a bounty). Neither slaves of loyal citizens nor slaves of Rebel or disloyal masters would actually

be free until the expiration of military service. These were instructions directly from Abraham Lincoln as stated in a letter from Stanton to George L. Stearns, September 16, 1863, *O.R.*, 3rd ser., 3:816; *Nashville Daily Times and True Union*, February 27, 1864. See also Cornish, *The Sable Arm*, 237; Berlin, Reidy, and Rowland, *The Black Military Experience*, 122–26; Stephen V. Ash, *Middle Tennessee Society Transformed, 1860–1870: War and Peace in the Upper South* (Baton Rouge: Louisiana State University Press, 1988); and Benjamin Franklin Cooling, *Fort Donelson's Legacy: War and Society in Kentucky and Tennessee, 1862–1863* (Knoxville: University of Tennessee Press, 1997).

38. Albert Castel, "'Captain, We Will Meet You on the Other Shore': The Story of Some Black Union Soldiers from Georgia As Told by a White Union Officer from Michigan," *Georgia Historical Quarterly* 87 (Summer 2003): 275–96.

39. Trudeau, *Like Men of War*, 336–37, 276–77. The First Colored Brigade included the Fourteenth, Sixteenth, Seventeenth, Eighteenth, and Forty-fourth USCT.

40. Trudeau, *Like Men of War*, 345. See also Anne J. Bailey, *The Chessboard of War: Sherman and Hood in the Autumn Campaigns of 1864* (Lincoln: University of Nebraska Press, 2000), 132–68.

41. Trudeau, *Like Men of War*, 344–46. See also Anne J. Bailey, "The USCT in the Confederate Heartland," in Smith, *Black Soldiers in Blue*, 227–48; Report of James T. Holtzclaw, January 12, 1865, *O.R.*, vol. 45, pt. 1, 705; Wiley Sword, *The Confederacy's Last Hurrah: Spring Hill, Franklin, and Nashville* (Lawrence: University Press of Kansas, 1992), 362–63; and James Lee McDonough, *Nashville: The Western Confederacy's Final Gamble* (Knoxville: University of Tennessee Press, 2004).

42. William T. Sherman to Spooner, July 30, 1864.

43. Mussey to [Foster?], August 2, 1864.

44. Lincoln also told Sherman: "It is not for the War Department, or myself, to restrain, or modify the law in it's [*sic*] execution, further than actual necessity may require. . . . We here, will do what we consistently can to save you from difficulties arising out of it." Abraham Lincoln to William T. Sherman, July 18, 1864, in *The Collected Works of Abraham Lincoln*, ed. Roy Basler, 9 vols. (New Brunswick: Rutgers University Press, 1953), 7:449–50. See also William T. Sherman to William M. McPherson, [ca. September 1864], Sherman Papers, Huntington Library, San Marino, Calif., quoted in Fellman, "Lincoln and Sherman," 146; William T. Sherman to Halleck, September 4, 1864, *O.R.*, vol. 38, pt. 5, 792–93; Thomas to William T. Sherman, June 20, 1864, *O.R.*, vol. 38, pt. 4, 542–43; Thomas to William T. Sherman, June 22, 1864, *O.R.*, vol. 38, pt. 4, 571–72; Thomas to William T. Sherman, June 19, 1864, *O.R.*, 3rd ser., 4:436 (same

as June 20 letter); and Michael Fellman, *Citizen Sherman: A Life of William Tecumseh Sherman* (New York: Random House, 1995), 158–60. Thomas also told the secretary of war that he thought Sherman's threat to arrest recruiters was "especially harsh." Thomas to Stanton, June 15, 1864, *O.R.*, 3rd ser., 4:433–34.

45. William T. Sherman to Lincoln, July 21, 1864, *O.R.*, vol. 38, pt. 5, 210; William T. Sherman to Spooner, July 30, 1864. See also two letters, both William T. Sherman to Halleck, July 14, 1864, *O.R.*, vol. 38, pt. 5, 136–37. The quote is from the second letter, received on the fifteenth, where Sherman told Halleck that he would not permit recruiting, "and [he would] not have a set of fellows . . . hanging about on any such pretenses." See also Fellman, *Citizen Sherman*, 163; Joseph T. Glatthaar, *The March to the Sea and Beyond: Sherman's Troops in the Savannah and Carolina Campaigns* (New York: New York University Press, 1985), 57; and William T. Sherman, *Memoirs of General William T. Sherman*, 2 vols. (New York: Appleton, 1875), 2:248. The 110th USCT was organized at Pulaski in November 1863 as the Second Alabama Colored Infantry. Its designation had been changed to the 110th USCT on June 25, 1864. See *O.R.*, vol. 47, pt. 1, 48, 69, 238.

46. Richard E. Beringer, Herman Hattaway, Archer Jones, and William N. Still Jr., *Why the South Lost the Civil War* (Athens: University of Georgia Press, 1986), 371.

47. *Richmond Daily Examiner*, November 8, 1864; Hull, "Concerning the Emancipation," 143–69.

48. Smith, "Let Us All Be Grateful," 42.

49. See Jeffrey Wm. Hunt, *The Last Battle of the Civil War: Palmetto Ranch* (Austin: University of Texas Press, 2002); Phillip Thomas Tucker, *The Final Fury: Palmito Ranch, the Last Battle of the Civil War* (Mechanicsburg, Pa.: Stackpole Books, 2001); and James A. Irby, *Backdoor at Bagdad: The Civil War on the Rio Grande* (El Paso: Texas Western Press, 1977). There is no agreement on the correct spelling of the last battle of the Civil War.

50. Castel, "Captain."

INDEX

and a new life—often to be persecuted by Yankee soldiers and, if captured, punished severely by Rebels.

Anne J. Bailey is a professor of history at Georgia College and State University. Her many books include *War and Ruin* and *The Chessboard of War*.